Far from Home

a memoir

Far from Home

a memoir

Antoinette Kennedy

FUZE
PUBLISHING
Ashland, Oregon

Book design by Ray Rhamey

ISBN 978-0-9998089-0-0

Library of Congress Control Number: 2018930968

In memory of

James Charles Kennedy
Marjorie Warnick Kennedy
William E. Hayes, S. J.

Acknowledgments

Writing this book has been a personal odyssey, but I have not traveled alone.

Because of her tenacious commitment to excellence and to the art of the question, Molly Best Tinsley, my Fuze editor, helped this book attain a depth I could not have imagined.

Greg Chaimov, Marjorie Ille, and Alan Kennedy have been with me from the book's beginning, offering friendship, ongoing feedback, and limitless patience. Thanks, also, to the readers who critiqued early drafts: Shirley Abbott, Judith Brandt, Catherine Elia, Nicole Foran, Nancy Haught, Judith Kelly-Quaempts, Deborah Lincoln, Sara Salvi, and Chris and Barbara Westover.

I owe more than I can say to Amy Shelly for her invaluable, creative assistance with social media. My thanks extends to Chris Santella who offered insights into the marketing world.

Thank you to the many—too long a list for this page—who have supported me over the years. My deepest gratitude goes to Mary Boucher, and Alan Kennedy and Michael

Kennedy, who share my family, but have their own unique memories. Thank you, dear sister and brothers, for encouraging me to share mine.

Contents

Preface

One wears jeans and sweatshirt on a Habitat for Humanity project. Another, in a blue suit, teaches inmates at a women's prison. The woman in white blouse and black skirt encourages a gathering of local Gambian women to vaccinate their children, and the lady in Kate Spade eye glasses and lab coat is a cancer researcher. The artist at work in her studio and the woman driving a tractor live in a cloistered community whose home is wide open to visitors. The one in gray pantsuit and colored scarf sits in dialogue with a Goldman Sachs CEO. These women are today's Catholic nuns, and their roles have expanded beyond narrow stereotypes of the "good sister" or the fierce disciplinarian. Whether in contemplative or active congregations, nuns engage with their urban, suburban, and rural communities. Their enclosure includes the whole world.

My story recalls a different time.

I lived in the convent before *The Sound of Music* and *Call the Midwife* invited viewers behind the walls, and my experience of the Catholic culture of the 1950s and early 1960s was far more complex than a musical or a Public Broadcasting Service series. It began with the limited choices available to young women at the time: in athletics, the primary sport for females was cheerleading; beyond school there was no Peace Corps, VISTA, or Teach for America. What society had to offer a woman was marriage—the chance to put her requisite home economics courses to work. Even college was considered primarily as an opportunity for "ladies" to gain their MRS degrees.

In a pragmatic sense, the convent was a viable career path, the chance for a Catholic woman to serve God and country outside the domestic arena. Once she became part of a religious order, her choices multiplied. For her work in schools, hospitals, and orphanages throughout the world, the Church offered the religious sister financial security. Because she sacrificed family to serve others, the Catholic nun also was given a level of admiration and respect, if sometimes only grudgingly.

As a Catholic child of a traditional community, I found a certain appeal in religious life. John F. Kennedy had challenged my generation, "Ask not what your country can do for you—ask what you can do for your country." The Church had added her own expectations: love God, serve others, and be faithful to His call.

Even though we Catholics had been raised around "sisters" or "nuns," they remained mysterious creatures behind white caps, black veils, and flowing habits. We never saw them eat or swim or excuse themselves to go to the bathroom. We did know, however, the three ways open to a

Catholic woman who longed for heaven: religious life, marriage, or the single life. Ranked highest, the nuns were God's favorites.

With five other women, I joined the Sisters of St. Francis of Philadelphia, West Coast Province, in 1961. Our three-year initiation, or novitiate, occurred at Our Lady of Angels Convent in Portland, Oregon. During the first phase, our postulant year, we wore simple black dresses and shoulder-length veils and learned to walk, under the guidance of the novice mistress, through the maze of appropriate external behaviors. Through study, prayer, and daily responsibilities, our task was to examine whether or not this was the life to which God had called us.

During the second or canonical year, our dress was the black habit and a white veil, and our task was to dedicate ourselves to theology, the Rule, prayer, and a powerful dose of manual labor. The period was another opportunity for novices and superiors to assess our call to religious life.

The third stage, that of a second-year novice, required more than work, study, and prayer. The novice prepared for her first mission assignment—whether in the classroom, hospital, or orphanage. More importantly, she discerned, with the help of the novice mistress, her readiness to profess first vows: to live poverty, chastity, and obedience for one year.

Why, the one year? The community, in its wisdom, realized the novitiate was not enough time for a young woman to make a pledge for life. After first profession, we renewed our promises at intervals for the next six years. At last, at the end of a nine-year preparation, we professed final vows—a promise to God and the congregation that we would be faithful to our commitment until death.

My memoir follows a distinct pattern. To illuminate the experience of religious life, which no doubt is foreign to many readers, I have developed each chapter around excerpts from the now antiquated *Franciscan Constitutions and Rule*. Its admonitions governed my life for twenty-four years. Both inspiration and directive, they prescribed specific actions and demanded a commitment to perfection. Each chapter recalls family influences, and reports how, as a young woman, eager to serve, I brought a conflicted but intense desire to answer God's call. Each chapter ends with reflections on how this desire shaped me and at what cost.

By choosing the convent, I believed I was following God's will, but religious life enclosed me in unsettling opposites: it was inspiring and safe, but exacting and confining. Restless and unsure as I was, I professed first vows, renewed these promises, and made final vows in 1970. I stayed for fifteen years more before leaving the Franciscans in 1985.

Far from Home is an invitation to go back in history to a more innocent and less cynical time when most young women chose marriage and motherhood. With a similar sense of the preordained, I entered the convent.

Today that choice may seem strange, even incomprehensible, but if you travel with me, at some point you may discover a familiarity, a kinship. You might remember promises made in youthful idealism, promises that, years later, you could no longer keep. You might say, "Yes, I've been there, too." If that happens, my journey, though unique, is no longer a solitary one. Together, we can share memories of flight and freedom, and even in the dark, find our way back home.

Route

Taking any route, starting from anywhere,
At any time or at any season,
It would always be the same . . .

                    T.S. Eliot, "Little Gidding"

Answer the Call

That they give clear evidence of a good will and read-iness to do whatever is calculated to make them use-ful members of the Community.

That morning in the nuns' new chapel, light bathed the altar, gold tabernacle, flaming candles, and tulip bou-quets. It shimmered through the stained-glass windows, glanced off the wood statues, and rested upon the young Jesuit standing on the altar steps. He shone, too: dark hair, dark eyes, black suit, and shoes. He smiled at us, and I felt an excitement bubble up and spread through the chapel, all the way to the back where the Infant of Prague statue stood in gold robes.

It was 1960, and according to annual tradition, the Fran-ciscan sisters had invited a visiting Jesuit to lead a three-day silent retreat at the high school. In place of classes, we gathered in the chapel for lectures, Mass, and the rosary. We walked the school grounds alone to think and pray. The ob-jective was not only to encourage Catholic citizenship, but also to recruit young people to religious life, with a special emphasis on the Franciscan sisters for young women and the Jesuit priests for young men.

Both of these religious orders were familiar to us. Every school day, we climbed the concrete steps to the brick building that was St. Joseph's Academy, where the nuns presided over classrooms from first to twelfth grade. Two blocks east was St. Anthony Hospital where the white-robed Franciscans cared for the sick and delivered generations of Catholic babies who grew up to attend the Academy. One half-mile west from the school stood the stone structure of St. Mary's Church, where the Jesuit priests celebrated Mass, married Catholics, baptized their babies, and listened to parents promise before Almighty God that they would raise their children as devout Catholics. Priests chaperoned roller skating parties, the Catholic Youth Organization, drama club, and the Friday night dances. The students at St. Joseph's Academy had a rich but restricted social and spiritual life governed by the Franciscan nuns and the Jesuit priests.

That year our retreat master, Father William Hayes, was in a class all his own. Young, urbane, witty, he spoke of a Jewish Jesus Christ—the charismatic Son of God—who ate with sinners and challenged the powerful. Infatuated with this priest and awed by his energy, I laughed at his jokes, listened to the story of his own call to the priesthood, and delighted in the love he showed for his Jesuit brothers. Without coercion he opened up the possibility of a different future: a future other than college, or the inevitability of early marriage and babies. "During this retreat, think about what you want to do with your life," Father Hayes said. "Ask if God is calling you to be a nun or priest." For three days I did that.

Of course, I had considered joining the convent. What Catholic girl hadn't? I liked the quiet of the chapel where I could pray during lunchtime. I knew some super nuns, like my fifth-grade teacher in Eugene, Oregon. Strict, beautiful Sister Stella Maris—Star of the Sea. In Pendleton, where I'd lived since sixth grade, there was Sister Noreen with the violet eyes, Sister Joseph Therese who moderated our cheerleading squad, and Sister Imelda Joseph who had turned our chorus into a champion. How keen was it that the nuns waited up for carloads of kids to drive by the school (where the nuns lived on the third floor) and honk out another basketball victory? What would prom night have been without a side trip to the convent parlor to show off our formals and tuxedos?

But joining the convent seemed a stretch. I had a boyfriend who was sweet and smart, a cute athlete with a blond crew cut and a smile that made his blue eyes crinkle. From a good Catholic family as well, he had two brothers preparing to be Jesuits. He was fun and easy to be with, a good dancer, and he loved me—even though I'd said I didn't want marriage and babies anytime soon and sure didn't plan to live in Pendleton (where the main draw was the annual September Round-Up) for the rest of my life.

I had dreams. I wanted to be an artist, a magazine illustrator. I filled sketch books with beautiful faces, their bone structure like Marlene Dietrich's. I imagined a New York career, and the highlight of my fantasy? Stopping by the dentist's office and picking up a *McCall's* or *Collier's* and find-ing, next to the short story, my colored illustration of the hero and heroine, and my name written on the bottom corner.

Besides, my father would never agree to my joining the convent. In second grade in Eugene, the nun dressed me like Mother Mary Rose, the founder of the Holy Names Sisters. I wore the black habit, cap, white starched blinders, and black veil. Nun for a day, I hopped in and out of classrooms, de-lighted, not simply because of the applause, but because of the escape from arithmetic class. A sister whispered, "Maybe you'll be one of us someday." When she added, "Wouldn't your father be proud?" I already knew the answer, but didn't tell her.

The religious life was no place for a daughter of his. Ada-mant in his opposition, he discounted the Church's insistence that a vocation brought blessings to the parents. A man of contradictions, though, he kept close ties to nuns and priests. In his Eugene private practice, he was the personal physician not only to the Holy Names Sisters, but to the bishop of the diocese, and he boasted about his brother, Alan, who joined the priesthood after serving in World War II.

Clergy visited our house more often than my friends, and my father's best friend was Father Hurley, a Jesuit from St. Andrew's Indian Mission, located a few miles outside Pendleton. The medical community joked that during St. Anthony Hospital parties, Dr. Charles Kennedy left his col-leagues to join the Irish nuns in the kitchen. He liked the nuns, but didn't want his daughter to become one. "You've got your whole life ahead of you, kiddo."

When he heard Father Hayes would stay for another five weeks to help in the parish, my father made sure the young Jesuit was a regular guest in our house. Not only did Father Hayes play golf with us, he shared our candlelight dinners where he and my father talked of Notre Dame and Senator John F. Kennedy and Ireland.

"What do you think of Father Hayes?" I asked him one night.

He responded, "A fine chap."

I took that as permission to claim dibs on this priest. I began attending the 6:30 morning Mass at St. Mary's— the super holy folks and smitten me. One morning, Father Hayes and I stood outside the church. His face brightened when he talked about taking his final vows as a Jesuit.

I asked, "What if I enter the convent and I'm not happy?"

"Happiness never lasts, Toni. Only God can satisfy you."

On the Sunday Father Hayes was to leave for Spokane, the parishioners stayed after Mass to see him off. I watched for a break in the line, sure of a special goodbye. Father Hayes smiled and shook my hand. "I'll be praying for you, Toni."

He turned away, his attention on someone else. Disappointment flooded me. I had so many things I wanted to tell him, especially the new plan: if God called, I wouldn't refuse. In the back of my mind I stored other imaginings. If I were a nun, Father Hayes and I could play golf or maybe go to Africa together. Or Molokai. He would bless the lepers and I would wrap their wounds. We would be friends forever.

With my dear Jesuit gone, it did not take long for my desire to burn low. To rekindle enthusiasm, I attended another retreat, a weekend with eight other girls at Our Lady of Angels Convent set high in the southwest hills of Portland, Oregon. We ate fresh bread and cinnamon rolls, roast beef and mashed potatoes. We listened as the sisters sang and prayed aloud the psalms. We laughed late at night, garbed in towels to look like nuns.

During that May retreat the fervor returned. Not because of the food, young nuns, or the other high school girls, but because of the convent on Palatine Hill. I fell in love with the ivy-covered mansion, the Victorian parlor, the library smelling of leather and wood, the chapel of marble and stained glass, the arched brick cloister walks, the sweep of lawn running down to the novitiate building, the grounds where azaleas and plum trees blossomed, and the Douglas firs rising like a fortress against the outside world. How I yearned to live in a place like that.

In the foyer of the main house hung a large oil painting. The rendering possessed a Venetian sense of closeness, rich color, heavy fabric, all the qualities part of the artist's vision interwoven into a biblical narrative.

Jesus, one hand outstretched in invitation, stood near a young man. The young man, head angled away from Christ, was dressed in fur-trimmed velvet, with brown leather gloves and beret. In the Bible story, when Jesus told the man that if he truly wanted to be perfect, he needed to give up everything, the youth turned away because he had treasured possessions. God summoned him and he said, "No."

As I stood in front of the painting, I asked God if He was calling me.

I returned home, outwardly excited about the retreat, inwardly anxious about a vocation to religious life. My mother asked for details. My father was silent.

From June through the end of the year, I stopped talking about being a sister, but I found a book in the library and read about religious orders of the United States. The text described the history, work, and mission of many different congregations, like the Dominican and Providence Sisters, the Sisters of St. Joseph and Notre Dame, the Holy Names and the Franciscans. Which one would I choose? I flipped back again and again to the photo of the pretty nun in white starched cap and celluloid collar, a black veil floating atop the white starched one. Her pleated habit fell elegantly and the white cord with three vow knots accentuated her slim waist. Which one? Probably, it would be the Franciscan nuns in Pendleton. They had the prettiest habit.

Before Christmas, my father, mother, my brother Alan, and I sat in the living room, listening to Bing Crosby croon "White Christmas" while embers crackled in the fireplace. My father reached for his wine glass, but his hand slipped, and the wine spilled onto the green shag carpet. The familiar alcohol odor of his breath spread into the air. His face looked drawn, and when he got up from the chair, his leg moved strangely. That night, fear snatched at me—fear for my melancholic father, Phi Beta Kappa, the brilliant physician who self-medicated with prescription drugs and wine. Late in the night, I awakened and crept down the hallway toward my parents' room—the inner sanctum we were not allowed to enter.

My father's voice sounded small. "Mommy, I can't move my right side."

We celebrated Christmas in the hospital. A miniature artificial tree stood at an angle on the window ledge. As sick as my father was, he never failed to smile when the nuns dropped by to check on him. Old Sister Leonidas, who probably delivered most of the kids at St. Joseph's, soothed him with her Irish brogue, and young Sister Lucy set aside her lab technician duties to spend time at his bedside. Three weeks later he was well enough to go home.

During the first months of 1961, life didn't hold much happiness for any of us. The stroke paralyzed my father's right side, impaired his speech, and tore at his pride. Our family closed in upon itself. When my mother, tired from too little sleep and worried about finances, said, "Toni, you are the only one who makes your father smile," the responsibility seemed more burden than blessing. If earlier a direction had been clear because of a handsome Jesuit, my father's illness limited my decisions. I put sketch books and colored pencils into a box and shoved them in the back of the bedroom closet. Days passed and reduced my future to my father's disability and a life trapped in Pendleton.

The nuns wanted me, though, especially the chorus teacher, a gifted, dominant woman. I tried not to resent her hovering.

"I haven't seen you for a while, Toni."

"I've been really busy, Sister."

"We are praying for your father."

"Thank you, Sister."

"Do you still plan to join us?"

"I don't know, Sister."

"Toni, if God is calling and you refuse, you'll never be happy."

In February I entered the cool, dark enclave of St. Mary's Church. It was Lent and the statues hid under great swaths of purple cloth. At the back was a prayer niche of wrought iron and glass votive candles. I knelt on the cushioned prie-dieu, dropped a nickel into the offering box, and when I lit a candle, the red glass twinkled. A raunchy basketball cheer we had been choreographing ran through my head. *Satisfied. Are you satisfied?* How could I be with illness, a tired mother, no college money, and a boyfriend I'd avoided?

Trying to pray, I lifted my eyes to the crucifix suspended above the candles—to the figure of the God Made Man, whose suffering made my trials seem insignificant. At once, a halo encircled Jesus on the cross. Light expanded and pulled at my desire to be generous, to open my heart to God's will, and to give myself without reserve. "Are you calling me?" I asked aloud. Close to me, the candles pulsed, seemingly with God's response, and I decided right there, beneath the cruci-fix, that I would enter the convent.

Out from a corner of my soul crept a darker reality, one tinged with relief and guilt: I had an excuse and a way to leave home.

I spent a lonely summer cut off from friends. Mostly I stayed around the house with my father. With some of his mobility regained, he began once more to rise early, and so we, father and daughter, renewed an old ritual: he knocked on my door and opened it a crack. I woke to see him holding on to his walker, his white shirt a little rumpled and his speech still a struggle. "Time to get up, Toni." Before daybreak, we sat at the dining room table. No longer was there a wine glass from the night before or Benzedrine pills for the morning, but he did continue to smoke, so Raleigh cigarettes and coffee stayed put.

One morning, two weeks before I was to enter the convent at Our Lady of Angels, I held a mug of chocolate close and watched my father slowly stir sugar (one, two, three teaspoons) into his creamy coffee. Then he spoke, asking the question I had anticipated and dreaded: "Why, for the love of Mike, Toni, do you want to be a nun?"

I was doing the unthinkable—joining the convent. Always, urging me on, was the experience of the darkened church and crucifix. Official papers were signed. Gifts from my mother's friends were piled in my bedroom—towels and washcloths, toothpaste and shampoo, white T-shirts and handkerchiefs. And the desire to escape tugging at me.

"It's too late to back out now, Daddy."

His eyes filled and his words came out haltingly. "Don't forget, kiddo. You can always come home."

In the 1990s, my siblings and I sat in my living room and watched an old home movie clip that Michael, my older brother, had converted to a video tape. Quick panning showed our white house, one of the residences provided for doctors who worked at Pendleton's Eastern Oregon State Hospital. Just outside the door stretched our own driving range.

We Kennedy kids, in jumpy black-and-white footage, took turns to tee up and hit the ball. Even though the clip doesn't show it, I imagined what a golf shot would have looked like: skimming the lawn, arcing south over the slope of the wide empty field, bouncing, gaining yardage, and disappearing into the weeds. The film granted each of us our moment. Mary at fifteen added the sweet pause at the top of her backswing, and Mike at thirteen possessed the easy grace of a Sam Snead. Eleven-year-old Toni swung long and smooth, but (uh, oh) lifted up on her toes. Alan, at nine, attacked the white sphere with quick, fierce determination.

But my father stole the show.

With a speed that defied truth, he teed up six balls, applied Ben Hogan's waggle, swung, and noted the flight briefly before hitting the next and the next. Watching the film, we laughed out loud. Alan said, "That's Dad." What the clip failed to capture was what occurred after the rapid-fire hits. Grabbing a bucket, he ran down the slope and up into the field, swooped up the balls, strode back across the lawn, and started again—sure that if he moved fast enough, and swung hard enough, he would execute a golf shot that would satisfy him.

The earlier memory of him in constant, restless motion is a sharper image than the later one of a crippled man. A relentless creature who strived for something more in a place called somewhere else—that was Charles Kennedy. An Irishman rarely contented, either with himself or others.

Even at eighty-two years of age, Father Bill Hayes was a man of humor and focus. In 2012 we shared lunch at an Italian restaurant close to Portland's Jesuit High School, where he had worked for thirty years and where he had the status of a legend. We munched garlic bread and spooned pasta. Dean Martin crooned "Volare," and the smell of parmesan blended with tomato and oregano. Around us plates clattered and silverware clinked. He still looked handsome in shades of gray and black, and when the young waitress fussed, his dark eyes twinkled. Slim, he possessed facial bones like Paul Newman and hands like a surgeon's. He sat back, relaxed, and talked about the new addition to the school, the students he loved, and Hayes Plaza, the outdoor courtyard that was named for him, but a space he dedicated to Mary, the Mother of God.

The young waitress approached us again. She filled our water glasses, smiled at one of us and then the other. Perhaps she wondered how long we had been married, or maybe we reminded her of her grandparents, even great-grandparents. Maybe she spoke loudly because we might have been hard of hearing. Father Hayes caught my eye and winked.

We bemoaned the distance lost on our fairway drives and how it was more fun to play the shorter courses. We talked about Obama and espionage novels, the Church's unbending stance on birth control, and the shameful crime of pedophilia. He spoke of his upcoming retirement.

"What kept you faithful all these years?" I asked him.

His response came without artifice. "I've had one prayer all my life, 'Jesus, have mercy.'"

How simple to have a focus like that. I envied him.

His gaze was kind. "Were you ever happy in religious life?"

I hesitated. "Probably the best years were in the novitiate. Afterward things pretty much fell apart."

"Do you know why?"

Here he sat, this inestimable man who had invited me to link satisfaction only with the infinite. I answered. "Nothing was ever good enough."

On a Wednesday morning in October of 2017, Bill was on my mind. The previous May I had visited with him at the Jesuit retirement center in Los Gatos, California. A month later, I sent him a copy of this memoir to make sure that my words about him did not offend. He called me back to say, "Actually, I'm quite flattered." Why was I so preoccupied with him that autumn morning? Even before I drank a cup of coffee, I sent him an email. In the afternoon I received a message telling me that Father Hayes had died the previous night at 10:21 p.m. of congestive heart failure. The message ended with "He spoke fondly of you, Toni."

We are mortal. We live in seasons of birth and death, joy and mourning. William Hayes was almost ninety years of age. He was ready. Yet I cried, sad that I had not written the card I had chosen for him. I had procrastinated, sure of more time. I reread the email, noting the time of his death, and all at once, recalled last night—the stark waking up. I had looked at the clock: 10:25. Not a voice or footsteps outside. I checked on my Shih Tzu, Angel, asleep on her pillow. *Strange*, I thought. *Wonder what woke me up?* I remembered settling into the covers and falling asleep instantly.

I knew then why I'd awakened, and some of my grief eased. So like him, my considerate Father William Hayes, gracious priest, to stop on his way home to say goodbye.

I had been awakened like that once before—forty years earlier. After my father's death in 1975, I continued graduate studies at St. Bonaventure University in New York. One morning, before daybreak, I broke out of a deep sleep to see my father—healthy and smiling, dressed impeccably in his white shirt, tie, and sweater vest—standing at the bedroom door. Light from the hallway framed him. "Time to get up, Toni," he said. Filled with a joy so intense, I pushed the covers back, ready to join him. Then the room went dark. Just a dream. Sorrow enters, passes through, but returns again.

Although my sadness comes from more than one direction, it does have a marker I recognize: I chose a path my father did not want me to travel. At age eighteen I listened to two heroes. A holy priest inspired me to imagine a different future, reinforcing my own search for a divine reason to travel far from home. Yearning to make an indelible mark upon the world, I left another man, my father, behind. What I have learned over the years is that blood ties stretch, but do not break. I may have left my father behind, but he did not leave me. I still possess his bone structure and metabolism, his anger and impatience, his unrealized dreams and his restless, discontented heart.

Take the Last Seat

That they not show singularity by having particular napkins, table service, table cloths, or anything of the kind.

In the dreamy land of memory, my sister, brothers, and I tiptoe down the first flight of stairs. Below, my father whispers and my mother laughs. We children sit on the landing, sure we are hidden. The pink sleeper pulls at my toes and the warm wooden banister pulses against my face. My father and mother dance slowly and gracefully, his cheek against her brown hair. As they glide and turn, his woolen slacks disappear and reappear in her flowered skirt and the Victrola plays, "I'll make a string of pearls out of the dew for you, for you . . ."

I hum. My father glances up. My mother stops. Both move apart. He stretches out his arms and I slip downstairs. He picks me up and holds me against his shoulder. On the first turn, my mother smiles, folds her hands in front of her, and watches us. My father's gray tweed jacket tickles my face.

He smells like King's Men and steak, cigarettes and wine. His hand, strong and slim, encloses my fingers. We turn round and round while he sings, "I'm gonna' dance with a dolly with a hole in her stockin' and her knees keep a knockin' and her toes keep a rockin'." I am special, a princess in the kingdom of my father.

When the Franciscan nuns at St. Joseph's Academy decided to have a student represent the high school (for the first time) in the competition for the 1960 Umatilla County Fair Queen, the nuns submitted my name (without asking). Unhappy with having to compete, knowing I would need a talent that would be different, I asked my father, "What am I going to do?"

"There's a poem that might work," he smiled, "given this horse-lovin' town."

From the shelf, he pulled a book, *The Best Loved Poems of the American People*, and read aloud Constance Fenimore Woolson's nineteenth-century classic, "Kentucky Belle." For fifteen minutes his voice transported me into the story of a young woman, the Civil War, a bone-weary, frightened Confederate soldier, and a cherished horse. In the two weeks I had to prepare, my father demonstrated how to use the voice as a magnet for attention. This poem would make me special.

The night of the competition, young high school girls from around the county danced and sang, played flute and piano. One of the last to take the stage, and the only one to recite a poem, I figured that I already had an edge. I waited for the shifting and coughing to end, and then I began to speak:

> *Summer of 'sixty-three, Sir, and Conrad was gone away—*
> *Gone to the county town, sir, to sell our first load of hay.*
> *We lived in the log house yonder, poor as ever you've seen;*
> *Roschen there was a baby and I was only nineteen.*

Immediately the audience was mine. They saw a woman dressed in calico, hands and face browned by sun. In the mystery that was theater, I'd become a young wife and mother, and I had a story to tell.

When the poem ended, the audience was absolutely still. Then the applause broke. The judges crowned me Queen of the Umatilla County Fair. The full-page spread in *The East Oregonian* delighted my mother and my father remarked, "It was the right poem for you, kiddo." No more talented than the other girls, I had chosen the unique (with the help of my father), and had been deemed the best.

For a full year our court shared talents and time with the county. Newspaper photos recorded our trips to local farms where we held squirming piglets, our visits to hospitals where the elderly smiled at us and applauded, and the parades where we rode in convertibles and waved gloved hands to family and friends.

Tiring performances in school auditoriums and Rotary and Elk lodges were balanced by fairground recitations under the stars, but one constant remained: when I held the audience in my palm, I was special.

The sense of privilege intensified with the decision to become a nun. No doubt I desired to do the noble act. Who wouldn't have considered an invitation from Father Hayes, prince that he was? Surely, I wanted to get out of Pendleton, and yes, I experienced a miserable summer of loneliness and regret for making the convent choice. Yet I wore this one belief bright as a tiara: the Franciscan nuns were pretty lucky to have me join them.

One afternoon in early September of 1961, I arrived three hours late to Our Lady of Angels Convent because I wanted to stop and visit with high school friends now at the Jesuit Novitiate in Sheridan, Oregon. The novice mistress, Sister John Aloysius, waited on the cloister walk with my set, five other young women who had been accepted into the Sisters of St. Francis of Philadelphia, West Coast Province. They had changed into their postulant garb. I wasn't wild about the ankle-length black serge dresses, and those Peter Pan collars were dated. I disliked how the veils looked with hair pulled back so that the ears showed. That was not a becoming style. I thought that I provided quite a contrast with my sun-bleached shoulder-length hair, red suit, and white gloves. "Don't be afraid to make an entrance," my mother often said. The novice mistress pulled a small gold pocket watch from under her white celluloid collar. "You will need to change now, Antoinette. Patricia will show you where." *I'll tell her later that I go by Toni*, I thought.

I followed the postulant into the novitiate building. One quick turn to the left and a series of cubicles (cells) appeared, all the same size, separated by plywood partitions and curtained entries. When I reached mine, I said, "I don't have a window."

Patricia whispered. "We have cells in the order of profession."

I planned to ask her what that meant later. For now, I had the shock of my new room. In place of my dressing table and gold-rimmed, attached mirror, there was a small nightstand with two drawers. Not a mirror in sight. No comfy cushions. A wooden chair. A narrow closet. No reading lamp, but overhead florescent tubes stretched end-to-end across the entire ceiling. A skinny bed and thin spread begged for my rose-flowered coverlet. And there on the bed rested my black dress and black stockings, and on the floor, black shoes. Slowly, I put on the postulant attire. Drawing back the curtain, I glanced around. At least the red suit and white gloves on the bed gave a little pizzazz to my space, but beyond that touch of color, no cell stood out. If I planned to feel special, it certainly would not be in the dormitory.

At dinner I discovered the meaning of order of profession. Where we sat at the table, in the community room, in chapel, and how we lined up from dawn to dusk depended on our arrival on Entrance Day. I may have made an entrance, but that choice had a downside. At the dinner table that night, I took the very last seat at one of the four rectangular tables with Formica countertops.

To help us out the first week, we postulants sat with Sister John Aloysius and a second-year novice whose eyes opened innocently one moment and twinkled in mischief the next. She seemed popular, so I made a note to be her friend. I planned to talk about my uncle, Father Alan Kennedy, pastor at St. Mary's Cathedral in Portland and a decorated war hero—Purple Heart, Bronze and Silver Star. I waited, but the sisters didn't talk. Silverware clinked against the white plates. Sister John Aloysius rang a small bell by her glass.

"*Benedicamus Domino.*"

In one voice the novices answered, "*Deo gratias.*"

At once, the sisters began to talk. I couldn't get a word in edgewise.

One of the postulants, tea pot in hand, offered to fill my cup.

I'd never had the stuff and didn't like the smell. "No, thank you."

The novice sitting across from me giggled before covering her mouth with a napkin. She leaned over and said, "We all drink tea."

I gave in, thinking *just this time.*

That night when I returned to my cell, it looked exactly like the other cubicles because the red suit and white gloves were gone. I pulled the curtain identical to the rest, then removed and hung up clothes patterned exactly after those of my set. I slipped into the white nightgown similar, I was sure, to every postulant. An identical kind of pillow supported my head and an identical blanket warmed me. Nothing to distinguish me yet, but I was pretty confident that, with a little Kennedy flair, I would set myself apart.

Although I hadn't had a chance to talk about Father Alan, a new opportunity popped up when Sister John Aloysius said, "Antoinette, you are wanted in the priest's dining room." Delighted, sure I was the first postulant to be invited, I entered the small room. Two large windows let in sunlight and a view of lawn and rhododendron. On the linen-covered table rested a bouquet of yellow mums, crystal goblets, china plates, cups and saucers, and real silverware. Bacon, fried potatoes, and scrambled eggs along with decanters of coffee and fresh orange juice showed that the priests ate pretty well.

Archbishop Power, who lived here at The Hill, nodded his dark head and smiled. Next to him stood our chaplain, skinny Father Juliano whose Mass vestments flew behind him like Zorro's cape. The other two priests, both stocky, one with hair, the other without, held out their hands. The bald priest, Father Campbell said, "Al's niece." He asked about my golf game and how I was "getting along." After a lovely chat, I excused myself, happy to have friends in high places.

When I returned to the kitchen, my set had already cleared the tables, washed most of the dishes, dried them, and set them in neat stacks. One of the postulants swept the floor. With a smidgeon of conceit and guilt, I whispered that I had been with the priests, but since we worked in silence, no one commented. A bit miffed, I thought, *I can't help it if the priests wanted to see me.*

So far, I had not endeared myself to the group (as my mother would say). When I learned that next week we would celebrate a postulant's birthday, I planned to make things right. Her birthday was also the feast of the Exaltation of the Holy Cross, and one of the novices helped me choose the perfect cake frosting. During study hall I worked on the words to a song, excited to lead the way—after all I had been a cheerleader.

In the novitiate music room, we began our practice. Teaching the catchy tune was easy because they had superb singing voices. The rest of the practice didn't go too well, even though I gave clear instructions when we snapped our fingers, where we clapped hands, and what was to be the highlight, the surprise action with the rosary.

Each time we sang the first line of the chorus, I wanted us to lift up the rosary and swirl it in a big, fast circle. "You know, how the '20s flappers swung their pearls," I said. "It will be a killer action." I thought maybe it was the cramped space, but the more I urged them on, the more their enthusiasm waned—maybe because they had attended all-girls high schools. I wasn't worried though. I figured they'd get into the spirit.

On the night of the celebration, we gathered in the novitiate community room. Already I sensed a festive atmosphere with the lights dimmed and tables pushed against the wall so that the twenty-six novices and the birthday postulant could be a real audience. The five of us postulants took our places in front. With a glance at my set and a one-two-three, we began to sing:

> *"I know a girl, one of our setta*
> *Hey Li Lee Li Lee Li Lo*
> *The Lord never made one any betta,*
> *Hey Li Lee Li Lee Li Lo."*

I sang loud, hoping to encourage the others. They joined

in, but I would have preferred a little more *oomph*, especially when we spun the rosary. The audience loved that part and laughed so hard they wiped their eyes. Even Sister John Aloysius smiled. I may have been last in order of profession, but I imagined Sister asking me to orchestrate all birthday celebrations from then on. I certainly had the knack.

Next morning after breakfast, Sister said, "I'll see you in my office, Antoinette." Eager to hear her compliments on the birthday party, I hurried through work, skipped out from the kitchen, along the cloister walk, through the enclosure, down the stairs to the dark hallway that led past the novitiate classrooms, and to the threshold of her office. I knocked.

"Come in, Antoinette."

"Thank you, Sister."

"You were called Toni out in the world?"

"Yes, Sister."

"Nicknames are not used here. We will call you Antoinette."

"Yes, Sister."

"Let us talk about the birthday celebration. It is good to see that you and your set are taking initiative."

"Thank you, Sister."

"Red frosting for the cake?"

"Yes, Sister. For the blood of Christ."

"What exactly was the name of the song you used?"

"*Hey Li Lee Li Lee Li Lee*. You know, The Limelighters."

"I'm not familiar with them. I thought your song was *Hi-Lili, Hi-Lo*."

"The beat's pretty slow on that one."

"We use songs that are less raucous. We do not want to give scandal to others."

"Yes, Sister."

"Whose idea was it to twirl the rosary beads like that?"

"Mine, Sister."

"The rosary is a sacramental, Antoinette. Next time, choose an action more in keeping with the spirit of religious life."

"Yes, Sister."

"Antoinette, do not seek to draw attention to yourself. Do not seek to be singular."

Singular? At this point in the conversation I realized that Sister may have smiled during the performance, but she did not like what I had done, and I would not be asked to organize birthday parties.

Sister said, "Do you know what to do now, Antoinette?"

"I'm not sure, Sister."

"Whenever we are corrected, we kneel to beg a penance."

Under her guidance and within eight days of becoming a postulant, I begged my first penance. I knelt on the floor, folded my hands and said, "I humbly beg a penance for being singular."

Sister nodded her approval and gave me a penance—a Hail Mary for the sick.

I kissed the floor. With Sister's dismissal, I stood, thanked her, and left the office.

Stung by her criticism, I crossed the hallway into the novitiate chapel. I nestled myself close to the window wall— the warmth of wood and the slight touch of air settled me. I wanted to have a role—my own—to play, but I wanted my set to like me. I considered apologizing to the birthday sister, but then again, maybe I should "hold my horses" as my father often said, and this awful regret would go away.

Before Sister John Aloysius could inform me that I was not allowed visitors, relatives arrived. Although I questioned why, during the first week, I was the sole postulant who had company, I liked getting out of hauling laundry baskets or sweeping stairs.

After saying goodbye to my grandmother and aunt, I headed for the brick cloister walk by the kitchen, ready to help slice apples, and opened the door. The air smelled of fruit and cinnamon. Stainless steel counters reflected light. No one was there, but huge pots of applesauce cooled on the gas stove. In the paring room, there were no peel scraps on the floor, no aprons left out, and no sound except the hum from the walk-in refrigerator.

Outside, close to the novitiate building, two postulants strolled across the lawn near the orchard. Eyes cast down, rosary beads dangling from their fingers—work completed, prayers rising to God—they were going on without me.

I had entered community pretty sure I would be one of a kind; sure that I would initiate new ways. Here I was, though, a dancer, dressed in black, spinning, spinning, all alone. A bird called in the distance and another answered. Back and forth bird-talk until I felt the dark mood lift. No postulants in sight now. I wanted to be unique, but not like this—not left out. If I hoped to be part of this community, I would have to do the hard work of change, and that singular act had to be done all by myself.

These days I keep on my writing desk a little flip chart of Eckhart Tolle's sayings from *A New Earth*. Every three months, I meditate on the reminder that if we want to be one with the universe, we need to be content not to stand out. A month later, a similar directive appears: if we are not careful, the ego shows itself in the desire to be special. Tolle offers a contemporary version of the imperative I learned as a postulant: "No sister shall show singularity by having particular napkins, table service, table cloths, or anything of the kind." In the past, I had tried perpetually to root out my imperfection. Now, a littler wiser, I don't fuss as much over how to change. Life takes care of that. The spotlight blows, or a puppy wanders in to steal the show. Sometimes (painfully) I face how wondrous a scene could have been without interruption. Life puts me in my place.

From 1980 until 1982, I shared community with four other sisters in a downtown hotel called The Rich. Newly renovated with city and federal funds, the second-floor area was termed an SRO, or "single-room occupancy": individual rooms with a bed, sink, and closet, as well as common spaces for the kitchen and bathroom.

We nuns were part of an innovative plan to provide low-cost housing to the poor in Portland's Skid Road. Our desire was to be sisters to the residents—all men—some of them recovering alcoholics, ex-offenders, and the mentally ill.

Each man had his own story and Tom was no exception. Years ago he possessed a sterling resume: researcher at Brookings Institute, chief economist for a major bank, author with his book registered in the Library of Congress, a husband, and a father. He lost his reputation, job, wife, and children. Lithium controlled his manic depression, but his days consisted of wandering the hallways, helping with the church clothes closet, and shrewdly observing the rest of us.

One day Tom stopped me in the hallway. "So, Sister, I hear that you give haircuts."

"Yes." I checked his dark, greasy hair. "You want me to cut yours?"

"All right." He shuffled down the hall, his shoulders rounded, making him seem vulnerable and smaller than his six-foot frame.

Although I scarcely recall the actual haircut, I do remember taking full credit for his transformation: clean-shaven face and confident step, ironed shirts and straighter posture. I took the opportunity, once too often, to say how nice he looked. One morning he regarded me with eyes penetrating and taunting while a smile curved his lips. "Proud of ourselves for the haircut we gave, aren't we, Sister?"

Thus, the spotlight does blow up. For a brief period, Tom had let me preen. He did not consider me his "sister." He sized me up early on, bided his time, and with one shrewd remark, sat me in the last seat.

On an autumn evening in 2017, I watched *The Sound of Music* again and waited for my favorite scene: Maria, in her dress with pale green bodice and filmy, flowered skirt, dances with young Kurt.

Then the boy, sweet child, surrenders his place to the Captain, regal in black tux. No other dance scene compares to the graceful, gentle movement of their *Laendler*, his muted clap and her skip, the two of them bowing apart and coming together. They float with the music, enveloped in romance, and not a single interruption occurs to spoil the moment.

The movie ended. The young boy relinquishing his position reminded me of a little girl in pink pajamas dancing with her father, and the memory jarred. Seventy years later, I had an aha moment. I replayed that scene from long ago—as it should have been: I sit on the staircase. The bannister's wood is still warm. But I do not hum. I do not demand attention. Without interruption, my parents dance their own *Laendler*. They hold one another, his cheek against her brown hair.

Sitting perfectly still, and in the place where I need to be, I watch my parents dance.

Unredeemed creature that I am, I vacillate between being a common traveler happy with any stump for a seat and the woman who thinks she belongs at the head of the manor table. Some days though, after another *mea culpa* for this curse of singularity, I take a break. I dance with my Shih Tzu Angel around the living room, a slow dip and twirl to Floyd Cramer's "Last Date." Nothing like his piano to conjure images of

a filmy dress and a white-gloved regal partner. And delighted,
I kiss Angel's furry head and whisper, "The universe is still
pretty lucky to have us."

Be Catholic

That they have spent at least two years in the prac-
tice of the Catholic religion before being admitted as
postulants.

In a Vancouver Catholic orphanage, in 1909, seven-year-old Charlie Kennedy sat with his nine-year-old sister and five-year-old brother in a large chamber filled with long wooden tables and straight chairs. He wore a white shirt and dark short pants. His auburn hair, parted in the middle, was cut close.

Two black-robed nuns moved about the room, helping soothe those whose parents didn't show. Daniel Kennedy arrived, posture straight and blue eyes keen. White shirt, black tie, and single-breasted gray-tweed jacket would have marked him as successful if the cuffs hadn't been frayed. His shoes held a high polish, but the heels were worn. He set a basket of oranges on the table and sat across from his three children. Within minutes a nun appeared and as she did on visiting days, took the fruit, nodded her thanks to Mr.

Kennedy, and glided off. "Are you learning your catechism?" he asked the children, and thus began another visiting day. When the time together ended, Daniel patted each of them on the head and told them not to be a bother to the nuns.

Because of their mother's death from tuberculosis and the burdens placed upon their father, Charlie and his brother Wilson and sister Ann spent time, as many children at that time did, in a Catholic orphanage. For the five years of their stay, the children continued academic and religious studies which demanded memorization, especially the answers to questions in the *Baltimore Catechism*, the standard Catholic text first published in 1885:

Who made us?

God made us.

Why did God make us?

God made us to show forth His goodness and to share with us His everlasting happiness in heaven.

What must we do to gain the happiness of heaven?

To gain the happiness of heaven we must know, love, and serve God in this world.

From whom do we learn to know, love, and serve God?

We learn to know, love, and serve God from Jesus Christ, the Son of God, who teaches us through the Catholic Church.

The children received the sacraments of Confession and Holy Communion. They attended daily Mass, and as was expected, Charlie and Wilson served as altar boys, rising early to assist the priest. At the end of their orphanage stay, the children would not have missed out on any aspect of a traditional Catholic upbringing.

When I was a child, our family always arrived late for Sunday Mass. "Hop out," my father said, pulling up to the curb outside the church. "I'll see you inside." Other families sat together at Mass. Not the Kennedys. My father stood in the back near the vigil lights, ready to duck out for a smoke when the sermon began. As families processed to receive the Body of Christ, he did not join them, but at the end of Mass, he walked out with the congregation. Thus, in one way he did "see us inside."

I rarely questioned my father's actions, but that changed on a spring day in 1950 at St. Mary's Church in Eugene. With fifty classmates, I celebrated First Holy Communion. Among memories of a white satin dress, net veil, and Mary Jane shoes, among remembrances of flowers and white be-ribboned pews, is the sight of my father walking up the aisle, and kneeling at the altar rail with my mother and the other parents. If I had kept my head down and prayed like Sister told us, I wouldn't have seen him tuck his hands under the white cloth covering the altar rail. Everyone else folded their hands on top of the cloth. Why didn't he know where to put his hands? I closed my eyes and hoped nobody else had noticed.

Later that day I asked him why he had hidden his hands. "That's what we did when I served Mass," he told me. I wanted to say that that was ages ago. I wanted to ask why he didn't go to Communion with us on Sundays, like a good Catholic. But I kept quiet.

My father was silent with regard to his relationship with God and Catholicism. He did not follow the rules. He did not pray the rosary. He did not go to Confession—even though he had a good joke about the subject:

Father O'Donnell listens impatiently to the woman relating her sin. A knock comes on the confessional door. Father interrupts the woman. "Phone call for me. Go to your pew and wait." Within minutes he's back. He looks out over the sinners and shouts in a brogue straight from the Emerald Isle, "Now, where's the woman who stole the pot?"

And on Fridays, while my father ate steak and potatoes, the rest of the family ate tuna casserole or fish sticks, because everyone knew that eating meat on Friday was a mortal sin.

If he seemed orthodox in his admiration for Al Smith, the first Catholic to run for the presidency, if he listened faithfully to the radio broadcast of Bishop Fulton Sheen, my father could turn on a dime and be chief critic of Catholic misdeeds. School may have taught that the Pope was infallible, but my father made clear that Church leaders were responsible for a bundle of dark decisions. One evening, he, once again, substituted the traditional Grace before meals with Robert Burns' toast:

> *Some ha meat and canna eat.*
> *And some wad eat that want it.*
> *But we hae meat and we can eat*
> *And sae the Lord be thankit.*

Sometime during the meal he railed against Vatican riches, the selling of indulgences, and the Reformation. As I listened to him, I thought about how smart he was. He could recite poetry—with a brogue no less—and knew so much about history that maybe even teachers didn't know.

Given my attachment to my father, it was inevitable that questioning of Church laws began by the time I reached third grade. I recall the day I asserted myself in a classroom of a thoroughly Catholic nun and all-Catholic classmates. Sitting in rows of scratched-up wooden desks connected by a wrought-iron frame, we each held a jar of thick cream, pushed the lid tight and sloshed the jar up and down. I stirred mine with a wooden spoon until my hand burned up to the elbow. Although my actions seemed identical to my classmates as I lathered a saltine cracker and tasted homemade butter, my mind was elsewhere. I had something important to say.

While the other children churned and checked and spread yellow stuff, I raised my hand and when called on, announced, "My father said that Martin Luther had good reasons for leaving the Catholic Church." Sister's mouth opened and shut before she quickly drew our attention back to the butter. I looked around to the other children staring. I felt a bit triumphant, as though I'd been given a head start in a foot race.

Charles Kennedy, cradle Catholic, was the skeptic, while our mother, Marjorie Kennedy, the convert, was a woman of faith. Each night she entered the room I shared with my sister Mary. Above our bed was the Lindberg *Heilige Schutz-engel*, the painting of two children walking barefoot across a bridge. Dwarfed by a stern sky and soaring trees, swirling waters, and a glorious guardian angel, the children journeyed hand in hand. Beneath the painting, I folded my hands and recited with my mother, "Angel of God, my guardian dear, to whom God's love commits me here, ever this day be at my side, to light, to guard, to rule, and guide." I prayed for Pope Pius XXII and the bishops, for family and friends, for the conversion of Russia, and for all non-Catholics. But every night, when the silence settled in and I got quiet inside, I worried. My father was clever, but he wasn't Catholic. I asked, "What about Daddy?"

"Let your angel do the worrying for you," she said.

I fell asleep under the careful watch of an angel resembling Gregory Peck, and within the tender love of my mother, the convert, who, unlike her husband, was Catholic clear to the bone.

As I grew older, I still worried about my father, but considered some Church rules silly, like girls or women having to cover their heads in church. Later, as a teenager, questions dealt with what I considered unfair, like not being allowed to go to an Episcopalian wedding or my father's life in the orphanage. Although he spoke little about those years, I had read the *Classics Illustrated* version of *Jane Eyre*, and I guessed how lonely and awful that time must have been for him. Why would the nuns drag a little boy out of bed to serve Mass? And I wanted to know more about the oranges. One day I slipped the question in sideways. "Did you eat the oranges for breakfast or lunch?"

He said, "I don't remember eating the oranges."

"Where did they go?"

"The nuns and priests took them."

"That isn't fair!"

He paused then and chuckled. "I'm pulling your leg, kiddo."

I didn't know whether to believe him or not, but the nuns had no right to the fruit.

St. Mary's Church in Pendleton was a small, tight-knit community of two-parent households who contributed money and talents to the school, hospital, and parish, and who sat in the same pews Sunday after Sunday. It offered a comfortable predictability in a religion that prided itself on staying unchanged. But what about the woman who sat in the back pew on weekdays and at Sunday Mass?

In her early forties with short, wavy reddish-blond hair, she knelt alone. She never went to Communion and the parishioners knew why. Not only was she divorced, but she'd remarried, and according to Church teaching, she was living in mortal sin. Faithful attendance at Mass, and yet her exclusion from the banquet seemed like the stolen basket of oranges, terribly unfair.

Comparing the divorcee's plight with that of two others in the parish did not help. Up in the front pews sat two middle-aged spinsters, one on the left side and one on the right, one skinny as a stick and the other round as a bowling ball. They had not spoken to one another in years, and gossip whispered that the quarrel began over a man. Yet when people stood to go to the table of the Lord, the two ladies followed, one in one line, one in the other, and with hands folded, they knelt, holy as you please, on opposite sides of the Communion rail. No law stopped them, not even Jesus' words about reconciling with your brother (or sister) before you come to the altar.

I did not proclaim to classmates and to the nuns my disagreements with the Church. Even my father would have considered reticence the wiser choice. To be Catholic was, like our family life, a place of light and dark silences.

Once inside the cloistered walls of Our Lady of Angels Convent, I discovered a life free from contradictions. We six postulants had entered with identical, required documents: a written testimonial from the parish priest vouching for our good faith, piety, and unsullied reputation; certificates of Baptism and Confirmation as well as proof of freedom from marriage; and a certificate of health from a reputable physician.

Without exception, the Franciscans were united in obedience to Catholic teaching, the same teaching that never stuck with my father. God made us because he loves us and wants us to be happy in heaven; we gain eternal happiness when we know, love, and serve God; God teaches us through the one, holy, catholic, and apostolic Church; Jesus Christ was God and Man; He was born of the Virgin Mary; He rose—body and soul—from the dead; Jews and Communists needed to become Catholic if they wanted to go to heaven.

Like my father in the orphanage, we were awakened early in the morning. Quickly and without a mirror, we tossed on layers of clothing (union suit with an opening in the crotch, corset with fasteners for black stockings, chemise, dress, cape, veil, and Dr. Scholl's shoes). We stood in line, and when Sister John Aloysius rang the bell, we walked in procession—a skill acquired through years of lining up for Confession and Communion, the acquired knack of every good Catholic.

Inside the chapel, we dipped fingers in the holy water font and made the Sign of the Cross. We genuflected before entering the pew. And the Latin Mass was a language which we may not have understood completely, but could pronounce flawlessly.

The priest, his back to us, proclaimed he was going to God's altar (*Et introibo ad altari Dei*), and we answered, as orthodox followers, that God was the joy of our youth (*Ad Deum qui laetificat, juventutum meum*). We stood for the Gospel, knelt at the marble railing, and extended our tongues to receive the Body of Christ. No sister stood at the back and no sister refused to kneel and receive the sacred Bread. Once Mass ended, we processed down the aisle and out of church.

At meals, we prayed Grace (never the Robert Burns' version) and asked God to bless the food and bless us, the faithful. Instead of my father's jokes or questions, we listened to the stories of Catholic heroes. St. Rose of Lima cut her face so that she would be attractive to God alone. Father Isaac Jogues blessed the Iroquois as they cut off his fingers. Maria Goretti forgave her attacker as he stabbed her to death.

These stories we knew as well as we knew *Anne of Green Gables* or Nancy Drew. While my father might have told a joke about a saint's eccentric behavior ("that's a strange duck for you"), the convent held up each of these holy people as examples for our edification.

Weekly Confession was a ritual in which every sister participated. When my turn came, I knelt in the small, dark enclosure and folded my hands on the ledge. The aperture slid open, a faint odor of stale cigarette wafted through, the priest's profile appeared, and his raised hand shielded him from the penitent.

"Bless me, Father, for I have sinned," I whispered. The priest listened to my sins, absolved me, and gave me a penance of two Our Fathers. Like every other postulant and novice, I went to Confession, because we believed that acknowledging sinfulness not only purified the soul but readied the penitent for Holy Communion.

At night, each in our own cell, we knelt and prayed for our families, one another, and for the "grace of perseverance." Dormitory lights clicked on and off to signal "lights out." Once in bed with the covers pulled high, we waited for Sister John Aloysius.

A slight shuffle outside the curtain and then an arm, draped in black, reached in. A silver tube flashed. Sprinkles of holy water fell. No guardian angel shone down from a cell's bare wall, and no mother appeared to kiss us goodnight. Nevertheless, we did have a never-failing, gentle blessing from our mistress of novices.

To live without religious contradictions should have been difficult, for I was the daughter of a skeptic. But, for a while, I found relief in walking with others in a single, planned direction. In the place of doubt and worry, I had truth and peace. Being Catholic equaled certainty.

❧

In the late 1980s, a few years after I had left the convent, a former student came to visit. I sat across from her, noting the blond hair swept back in a chignon, the simple, elegant cut of her pale-yellow blouse, the long, tapered fingers, and the gentle manner.

"I still can see your editing marks on my papers," she said. "You taught me to write."

I smiled, happy with her memory. "Those were good days."

"Not all of them." She talked about her senior year, her older boyfriend, the pregnancy, her refusal to tell her parents or friends, the lonely trip to the clinic, and the terror and guilt of the abortion.

A terrible sadness clenched at my heart. "Why didn't you tell me?"

She shook her head. "You would have been the last person I would have told."

I wanted to justify myself, tell her that I would have understood, or at least now I wasn't the narrow person she had known. I wanted to tell her that I no longer believed in Hell, or the infallibility of the Pope, or that God devises ways to punish us. I wanted to quote the theologians who wrote that an informed conscience always trumps Church law. I wanted to say, "Don't you see? I've changed. I'm open-minded now."

"I'm so sorry," I said.

Her composed expression revealed my past righteous-
ness and rigid adherence to rules and law. Her eyes, though,
radiated a kindness and an understanding that I hadn't af-
forded her.

In 2003 the United States invaded Iraq and we were at war—
again. Lighting a candle, I sat on my bedroom floor, overwhelmed by anger and sadness. I thought of sick, ineffectual
Pope John Paul II, head bent, begging the world leaders not
to go to war. No one listened. I imagined beating fists against
politicians in blue suits, but aimed deeper rage, like a blow-
torch, at the silent, fearful American bishops. I mourned
the death of a Catholic Church I had once loved—that of
John XXIII and Daniel Berrigan, the nuns and priests who
marched at Selma, the missionaries martyred in El Salvador,
and Archbishop Romero who let the poor transform him. I
screamed inwardly at the modern-day clerics with soft hands,
riding in chauffeured limousines, hiding away, afraid of another pedophile lawsuit, no longer men of the Gospel. *You
cowards, how can you not speak up?* I wept for the Iraqi people,
for our soldiers, for a compromised Church, and at the ob-
scene war cry of "Shock and Awe." That night I said aloud,
"I am done."

Be Catholic. What exactly does that mean? "Once a Catholic, always a Catholic," my mother often said. Applied to my
life now, perhaps there's a grain of truth in her words, even
though I rarely attend Mass. Daily I pray with scripture. The
rosary slips through my fingers at night. Meat is not on my

Lenten Friday menus. I believe in everlasting life, the spirit world, and a guardian angel (no longer a movie star, just a simple, ever-present light).

Thanks to a mother and the Sisters of St. Francis, I am a believer of sorts, a woman in love with ritual: candle and incense, bread and wine, rosary beads and blessing water, silence and sacred spaces.

That is why, in 2012, on a trip to Russia, I visited St. Sergius Monastery, forty-five miles from Moscow. The gold domes, the basilica interior with frescoes, tombs, and icons offered welcome. Trinity Cathedral's candles and hanging lanterns sheathed the church in a subtle glow. Worshippers held candles and slowly walked toward St. Sergius' casket, all the while the pure *acapella* voices of the villagers rose in Russian chant. In this space of God, no camera flashed, no tune from an iPhone jingled, no chatter or laughter from the crowd. In the deep silence belonging to believers and the Russian Orthodox, I felt at home.

Those St. Sergius moments cannot last forever. Still my father's daughter, I am part heretic. If people loll about in the back of church, I smile to think that they plan to grab a smoke during the sermon. Those divorced and in a second marriage still sit in metaphorical back pews. In Portland, Warsaw, or Dublin, warring siblings worship apart from one another, an impatient priest hurries a penitent along, and in a darkened chapel kneels a lady who stole a pot. Martin Luther had more than one good reason for leaving Catholicism, as do those who seek compassion or justice and meet rejection or refusal.

Sometimes, though, when evening comes, I think of Gothic churches, built by the faithful placing stone upon stone over decades, grand massive structures where shadows play around arches and bell tower. Stained glass blushes with scarlet and gold, cerulean purple, and titian bright as a basket of fresh oranges. I imagine voices blending to pray evening song.

You brought me forth into a broad place;
You delivered me because you love me.
Yes, you light my lamp;
My God, you lighten my darkness.

A tiny yearning breaks through—to rest awhile in a simpler time of night prayers with my mother and morning psalms with convent sisters, all of us Catholic.

Do Your Share

That they be continually engaged in prayer and work, lest by unprofitable idleness, they open the door to sin.

According to my mother, I spent too much time with my head in the clouds. Unlike my sister Mary, who at age five cut a pattern and sewed a rust-colored velvet coat for her doll, and my brothers, who engaged in fort and airplane construction, I played with Wendy, a special sprite, who arrived the year I turned four. She lived in a real house that sat on the ledge above the fireplace. White with apple green shutters and matching green door, the home was tall as a picture book. One day I climbed on a step stool and peeked inside.

Two chairs upholstered with blue brocade and a white sofa circled a coffee table. Flowered throw rugs decorated shiny wood floors. On the dining table perched white tea cups with gold trim, spoons, and linen napkins. The writing desk with paper, feathered pen, and ink bottle stood to the right of the large picture window. A staircase wound to Wendy's bedroom where a brass bed, covered with a fluffy white comforter, rose to the ceiling. Wendy's open closet made my heart stop: silk and chiffon dresses of green, blue, and lavender. A velvet cape with matching gown blazed red as Santa's suit.

I climbed down from the chair, delighted with my discovery.

On a winter day, before my sixth birthday, Wendy's house disappeared from the mantel.

"How could she leave us?" I cried.

"She's gone to live with another family," my mother said.

"What will I do now?"

My mother, who never spoke down to her children said, "Cultivate a hobby, dear. The Devil finds work for idle hands."

Hoping to see Wendy again, I built a fairy garden made of moss and branches and set it against a Douglas fir in the woods behind our house. In a hole, I put a plastic bowl for a pond and hung a swing made of string and a piece of bark. A breeze passed by and I imagined fairy wings. In winter, I was sure the sprite skated over the pond in her white muff and fur-trimmed dress.

As the years passed, Mary added cooking and sewing to her list of talents, and Michael and Alan continued to build. I sketched and read romances, imagining a hero (directly out of Mary Stewart's gothic novels, like *Nine Coaches Waiting* and *My Brother Michael*), beckoning me into passion and adventure. I reveled in music like Percy Faith's "Theme from a

Summer Place" and wrote poems that had to rhyme: "Singing, softly singing, oh mystic violin/while low notes, sounds of summer, form a high pitched, swinging din." Idleness was my hobby.

Our Lady of Angels Convent introduced me to a life broken into half-hour segments devoted to prayer, meals, cleaning, study, and recreation. No time to jot poems in a red diary. The cells were off-limits except for sleep and during one's monthly period. "Upstairs Privileges" said it clearly: wasting moments in your room is not allowed; be swift with the Kotex change and come back among the sisters.

For most of the day I was kept more than occupied, but twice a day I learned the importance that the nuns (and my mother) placed on finding something constructive to do. After lunch and dinner, we postulants and novices congregated in the novitiate community room for recreation. At first, we sat in order of profession at long tables, at a specific spot, but once everyone was settled, we could move about and choose an activity.

On the first evening, I spent time looking out the row of windows that offered a tranquil view of the sloping south lawn, grape vineyard, and rhubarb plot. Soon enough, I turned my attention back to the community and watched, mesmerized by all the activity and surprised that my set was already engaged. A tiny, wiry novice—one of the ones who moved faster than I could think—motioned me over to an empty chair. Bright-eyed, with energy to burn, she asked, "Antoinette, how about helping out?" Together we unrolled her skein of yarn. Off to the side a sister's knitting needles produced the yoke of a little yellow dress.

Sister asked, "Have you ever knitted?"

I shook my head. "I crocheted a stole once." I flashed to the uncomfortable memory of the project. It was for my mother, who, in her gentle effort to steer me towards the useful, taught me how to form a slipknot. If I knew how to make a slipknot, I figured I could crochet a stole. Looking ahead to the holidays, I bought off-white yarn threaded through with bright gold. Impatient with the confusing instruction booklet, I struck out on my own. Month after month, I crocheted row after row, thinking, *in case it needs to be longer.* At Christmas, I watched my mother open her gift. She smiled and draped the stole around her once and then again. Bundled like a glittering snowball, she attended a hospital party—the one and only time she wore my gift.

The sister, as though she had read my mind, laughed. "I'll see that you have yarn."

My first contribution to the annual bazaar for the missions was a blue baby set. I applied chain and slip stitches, but was intent on getting the thing done and paid little attention to a consistent stitch. One of the Irish novices, who had finished an afghan beautiful enough for Aspen, teased, "The booties, bonnet, and sweater are made for three different children." True enough. Not being idle did not make for instant accomplishment.

Sister John Aloysius encouraged us, however, not to confuse idleness with leisure. Leisure is relaxation and is what ought to occur in the community room. The sin of the idle is not about enjoying well-earned rest, but about sloth and laziness. She reinforced this lesson with a St. Francis story. The saint saw a lazy brother feeding off the labors of the community and called him "Brother Fly." Sister explained what damage the idle person caused to herself and to the community as a whole.

Intrigued, I tried to understand the difference between leisure, work, and laziness. As the sisters tended to tasks, I watched them. Summer was a good time for observation when nuns arrived at The Hill, happy to help out after a year on mission. The Franciscan who tried to teach me math in high school would head, clippers in hand, for the narrow rose garden outside the novitiate building. She worked peacefully, pruning dead leaves, cutting the fresh roses into a cloth, and humming. Her task was not an obligation, but a joy.

Another teaching nun would arrive at The Hill and go immediately to the kitchen. She may have had her own apron, folded neatly, just waiting for her to pick it up and tie the strings. Her delight filled the place as surely as the aroma of melting butter. She laughed and joked, happy as a lark to have her sleeves rolled up and her hands dusted with flour, ready to spread gooey mixture of butter and cinnamon and walnut over the dough, and pop it into the oven. With the practicality of the seasoned, confident baker, she enjoyed her task and rewarded the rest of us.

And those with whom I lived? One novice in particular epitomized the unselfish act. She was the one who supplied my blue yarn, and she could cook and sew as well as knit. As soon as one task was finished, she moved on to the next, finding moments to help others dry the last of the dishes or sweep a final flight of stairs. At first, I figured she worked so fast, it was no wonder she could be many places at once, but gradually I saw that she possessed something more than just quick feet and hands. She was happy. I thought, *she likes what she does.* Her skills did not resemble work, but hobbies she had perfected and in which she found fulfillment. In sharing generously, she made our community that much richer.

Sister John Aloysius continued to offer lessons on idleness and its connection to community. The idle focused on their own comfort. The idle left messes for others to clean and refused to do their fair share. I didn't have a practical bent, but as I listened to her, a direction began to take shape: time is precious; in the moments given to me, I should decide activities I love to do and apply those skills unselfishly.

Family and God did not cut Sister John Aloysius and my mother from the same cloth. One was raised in the brick and mortar world of the east coast and one in the pioneer west. One was tall and dominant, the other small and genteel. One was protected by religious life and Catholicism and the other at the mercy of marital conflicts and financial insecurity.

Sister was distant and my mother affectionate. Yet these women, seemingly polar opposites, valued finding something constructive to do. Do not join the selfish idle who rip at the seams of love. Marjorie Kennedy began the process and Sister John Aloysius continued the education. They both advocated using moments wisely; only then do we have ample hours to be generous.

In trying to avoid idleness, I have allowed the terrier of busyness to nip at my ankles. I still tally in a little black book what I hope to accomplish each day—a blend of the spiritual, intellectual, and creative. I'm following the advice of the self-help gurus for the aging community: make friends, keep your mind and body occupied, get a dog, and cultivate an interest.

Creative unselfishness comes more naturally to my sister and brothers. Mary, magical seamstress of exquisite finger puppets and Christmas banners, crocheted snowflakes and calming quilts, wrote that "fabrics form their own landscapes. Laid flat, a silky surface ripples like water. Fluffed, a cotton piece forms mountains and gullies. Texture—nubby, smooth, satiny, grainy—add to the illusion of place." She has made the world of her children, friends, and the needy a better place.

Michael has built his own furniture that would make a Shaker craftsman proud: table, chairs, entertainment center, desk, and nook for his computer—to name a few items. If a neighbor needs a shelf or a planter box, there he is. Alan is not only a writer and meticulous editor, but a master at repair of his own home and a partner with his photographer wife. She snaps the camera, and he prepares the frames for exhibit. He builds the garden's raised platforms, and she tends the vegetables. If I were to say to any of my siblings, "You should have done this for a living," they would answer, "This is not a job. It's my project." They are much more the children of an artist mother than I am.

A few years before her death in 1991, my mother and I sipped coffee together in her quiet, cozy home in Pendleton. She had set out her maternal grandmother's white China cups trimmed in gold, white linen napkins, and a plate of chocolate fudge cut into delicate squares.

"This reminds me of Wendy," I said.

"Our fairy." She nodded.

"The inside was marvelous, mom."

"The inside?"

"I don't know how you did it. Sofa and chairs. The rugs. Tea cups like these. Her brass bed and clothes closet—all to scale."

My mother frowned slightly. "Toni, it was only a shoebox. I decorated the outside." Her face burst into a smile that made the years drop away. "Sweetheart, there wasn't anything inside."

Nothing inside. There we sat, two grown women: one of us delighted by imagination, the other tricked by an empty shoebox. Watching my mother, though, brought back memories of the sewing machine whirring in the night, of goblin and princess Halloween costumes, and a skirt for a high school dance. She cooked and cleaned and ironed out of duty, but she discovered ways to spend her best moments: creating magic in our unpredictable childhood.

I never learned to sew like Mary or work with wood like Michael and Alan, and I have not returned to novitiate days of knitting booties and hat, even though—on a whim—I got as far as buying lavender yarn and a bright red hook. One project, though, keeps the devil at bay, one that I never planned to cultivate. I like to cook. Not as a chef in a second career, no pining for all the years I refused to learn, but right now, as a hobby, as a way to be constructive and unselfish. If friends come for coffee, we can share homemade muffins: blueberry walnut bran and banana chocolate chip. Containers in the freezer hold chicken taco soup and layered chili casserole.

When the menu calls for lemon chicken, I brine the poultry the night before. The next day I slice each breast lengthwise and pound it into a ¼ inch thickness. When the pan is hot, I brown the pieces and the fresh lemon-chicken broth-butter-oil sauce makes them savory enough to melt in your mouth. In the sizzle, I hear my mother's approval. A long time coming, I know.

And now I've got a second project in mind. Right outside my patio is ground perfect for tending a Peace hybrid rose. I'll need to amend the clay soil and make sure the shade is partial. And I have a spray water bottle to take care of those pesky aphids.

A neighbor is sure to say, "Water? It's much quicker if you use that all-natural product."

I'll answer, "Oh, I have the leisure to do it the slow way."

If the plan turns out as I think it might, come summer the buds will burst into a salmon-colored glory, and the foliage will cradle the flowers in glossy green. Of course, I want people to smile as the fragrance wafts toward them, but I'm hoping for another visitor. Wouldn't it be magical if Wendy flew this way to dawdle for a while? In the impractical spirit world, no one cares how a fairy spends her hours.

Rejoice in the Good

*That they shall mutually honor one another, rejoice
with their whole heart in the good qualities of others
and do all they can to stifle the least germ of jealousy
in the Community.*

At the carnival I was a cowgirl in denim skirt and plaid
shirt, cowgirl boots and white cowgirl hat. My father
and I walked through crowds of shouting barkers and running children, past the Ferris wheel and bumper cars, the
Hall of Mirrors and the booth where, for a nickel, you could
toss bean bags into the clown's mouth and win a giant stuffed
panda. The smells of cotton candy and popcorn mixed with
hay and gasoline, wet paint and pigs. We reached the circle
platform, and the gate swung open.

"Which one?" my father asked.

The horses, caught in mid-leap, flamed silver and orange,
black and white. How very much I wanted to choose the
prettiest.

The man at the gate yelled, "Get on!"

My father lifted me onto the small pinto and said, "Hold tight." I slipped a bit on the brown saddle but grabbed the pole when gears shifted and the organ music vibrated and we moved up and down and round and round. The world outside blurred. Horses appeared to the side and in front—the gold palomino with the white mane and the black horse with the pink saddle. Best of all was a chestnut stallion with ivory stockings and turquoise tassels, clearly the prettiest horse, and someone else was getting to ride him.

Rather than pine for what we could not have, the Franciscan community expected us to rejoice in the talents of others. At first, that requirement seemed easy enough to follow. All six of us postulants were "born in legitimate wedlock, between the ages of 16 and 30; free from bodily defects, of unsullied reputations, in good physical and mental health, and in possession of middling talent." As I watched each member of my set, though, I realized that none of them fit in the category of a middling talent.

Small-boned and bespectacled Patricia, the first to arrive on entrance day, was the natural leader. She governed the sewing room where we crafted and mended items from white linen caps to black serge habits. The other girls possessed the necessary skills, but since I had rejected both mother and sister's sewing example, I needed Patricia's help to sew a chemise, the simple white undergarment that protected our skin from the serge. Patricia did not hover, but encouraged me as I smoothed the cloth, cut it along the grain, matched the seams, and pinned the pieces into place. She helped me with the needle and bobbin, and then moved away as I put pressure on the pedal. When I displayed the chemise on the table, Patricia checked the finished product and smiled. She moved quietly about the room, a patient, organized presence.

Kathleen's aquiline nose and deep set, sad eyes gave her the appearance of a Renaissance Madonna. She embodied my mother's belief that "anything worth doing is worth doing well." On our designated silver-polishing day, Kathleen meticulously cleaned the embossed vine and scalloped edge of spoons, knives, and forks. Her precision extended to salt and pepper shakers, coffee decanter, and sauceboat from the priests' dining room. The more slowly Kathleen worked, the more the odor of Wright's silver polish seemed to sting the air. *How long*, I grumbled inside, *before we could wash, dry, and store the pieces in blue velvety bags*? Sister Veronica Ann, in charge of the kitchen, stopped by, a smile on her face. "Kathleen, you are a wonder."

The novitiate community room welcomed Carol, whose domain occupied the small space of a card table. Bent close to the jigsaw puzzle, sleepy brown eyes magnified behind thick, square lenses, Carol's giggle warmed the room. Although puzzles had never been part of my childhood, I decided there was always a first time: I slid onto a chair and began to collect the small red pieces. Sister John Aloysius pointed to the box cover where the sky loomed large. "Start with the frame, Antoinette." Jarred by the correction and afraid mistakes would disturb the rhythm, I stayed away after that, but admired how the puzzle took shape: beneath the sky a rose bush climbed against the cottage, and a blossoming tree shadowed the chimney. Various sisters sat at the table, doing their part to finish the picture and cheered when the last pieces snapped into place. There was Carol, perfectly at ease in the heart of community.

On an afternoon in autumn, we postulants and novices sat silently in the Blue Parlor, located off the foyer in the main house. In this room decorated in blues and grays, stood the glossy, black grand piano. Our piano at home was a mahogany Chickering upright. Mary played a gentle *Humoresque*, Michael memorized sections of Tchaikovsky's *Piano Concerto No. 1*, and my mother faithfully returned to *Moonlight Sonata*. I plunked out my alto parts for chorus. My mother often told me, "You will regret all your life not learning how to play."

That day when we gathered in the convent parlor to hear Loretta play, I brought both limited experience and expectations. Once she took her place on the piano bench, my mundane mental wanderings vanished. She was no longer simply a postulant, but a pianist. Slender, stately, dark-haired, and dark-eyed, Loretta began to play, fingers lithe, wrists still. Memory recalls Sibelius' *Finlandia*, fine-boned hands lifted above the keys, the creation of drama and lilting melody, like a living entity, that resounded, leapt, trilled, and cascaded through the open doors. The music not only painted Finland's trees and water, ice and snow, but transformed the parlor and our black-and-white-world into shades of gold. Who had she become? The perfect image of a woman at home in her world of discipline, beauty, and skill.

Connie, the artist, seemed, at first, a kindred soul. Hadn't I kept notebooks filled with sketches? In the novitiate basement, off the library hallway, was a jack-of-all-trades room. On a day when the light was good, Connie was designing feast-day cards. Looking over her shoulder, I suggested a swish of more tissue paper and additional swirls of colored pencil. She smiled and shared her blank cards, but we worked separately. Alongside her sleek design, my creation seemed busy and scattered. I recalled giving my two cents' worth to my mother as she painted paper mâché Magi for the church bazaar. With Connie, I was again in the presence of an artist and still offering advice. An intrusion, not critical or arrogant, but an intrusion nevertheless. Connie had the artist's intuition: be aware of the moment when the simple becomes the cluttered. I did have the good sense to step away.

As much as I wanted to be happy for my set, I was envious. Where did I fit? What did I have to offer? I should have known, but the answer came as a surprise one evening, and fittingly enough, in front of an audience.

Besides the thirty-plus postulants and novices, other nuns lived at Our Lady of Angels Convent—the professed sisters who had made vows of poverty, celibacy, and obedience. Among these were retired nuns, administrators of our Western Province, grade and high school teachers, college students, and domestics. All of them ate in the professed dining room and each evening a postulant or novice was assigned to read there. Sister Theona, scholar and professor, chose the readings. Earlier in the week she had handed me an article from *America* magazine. As I practiced, I imagined my father, guiding the inflection, expression, diction, and delivery, warning me, "Don't get in the way of the words."

The article I prepared focused on the pending Second Vatican Council which was a gathering of Catholic bishops from around the world. As my father had taught, I waited until the sisters had settled. Then I began to read. It was like reciting "Kentucky Belle." With the audience attentive, my anxiety lessened and the words flowed, the narrative gained momentum, and the atmosphere in the room hummed with excitement. Vatican II would open the door to revolution. When I finished, many of the sisters looked up to smile. I made my way toward the exit, and one of the nuns whispered, "We want you back."

The weeks sped by and I settled into that first year of religious life. I tried not to glance sideways to compare myself with others, not to intrude into their spaces, and not to begrudge them their talents. Little by little, Patricia's order, Kathleen's work ethic, Carol's ease, Loretta's music, and Connie's artistry lost much of their threat. Mostly at peace, and pleased that others valued me as a reader, I tried to avoid that tricky "wistfulness" that left me feeling diminished.

One day before second semester, we novices and postulants sat in front of the gymnasium stage. Sister Joan, our education director, her hands dipping and flicking like wings, introduced a guest. "Sisters, we have with us today Cornelia Cerf, a dance professor at Marylhurst College. She will perform her choreographed work, entitled *Envy.*"

The heavy green curtain slid back, and the music began—wind instruments. In the center of the stage sat a coiled figure, dressed in green leotard and filmy green arm scarves. Slowly (seeming to move by millimeters), she

unwrapped herself. The music grew in intensity and so did
the dancer. She played with scarves as with living beings
meant to gratify and seduce. Raw energy vibrated through
her body—grasping fingers, treacherous rise and fall, hos-
tile hunch, foot bent and suspended in air, torso twisting
one direction and another, and the sudden, pouncing leaps.
With jagged gestures that her body carved into right angles,
the gargoyle danced in soft and luxurious green silk: envy
dressed as goodness and beauty.

Within Cornelia Cerf's first movements, I recognized
myself: the watcher on the lookout for the enemy, jaw set
and eyes narrowed, snatching at what was not mine.

At age fifty-seven, in the year 2000, I taught in a new school
but felt caught once more in an old maelstrom. At 3:15 the
students had left, but my head still throbbed from the noise
across the street from the classroom. For months construction had been underway to complete the Urban Planning
Center at Portland State University, leaving me with the endless vibrato of pile driving—the slam and crash and hammer. That afternoon, chaos swirled as a bus ground its way
past the window, workmen stomped, and freed teenagers
shrieked.

Turbulence continued indoors. The mother tapped her
pen, like a miniature jackhammer, on a notepad. Her daughter, flushed, brow tight, head bent, refused to look up. Her
left heel vibrated, and her leg jumped up and down, up and
down. The mother and daughter attended this meeting for

two reasons: to list my deficiencies as a teacher and to get a transfer out of the class.

I had arrived at the school sure of my ability. Assured that I had much to offer the students and teachers, I planned to excel and establish a reputation lasting all the way to retirement. And I wanted, more than anything, to end my career with that longed-for passion, a passion that would overwhelm, transform, and hang me like a moon in education's universe.

Instead, I faced defeat and writhed in envy. Students passionate about an "A+" (whether earned or not) infuriated me. A young girl, frightened by my impatience, ran out of the room. A hearing-impaired child complained when I did not provide daily written materials. The principal, gentlest of souls, had observed my classes to make sure no student was maligned. Exposed, I felt like the old days on the carousel, spinning round and round, clinging to the silver pole of dignity, and longing to be the English teacher two doors down the hall—the young one with the shoulder-length brown hair and spontaneous laugh, the one with the creative lesson plans and the literary smarts, the loving lady whom my students would have preferred as their English teacher.

That miserable first semester ended. I settled into my place as a freshman instructor who taught students to write. Surrounded by dedicated teachers and motivated young women, I might have found my passion. I did not. Have I ever wanted to excel enough—in teaching or in an artistic endeavor—to put in my 10,000 hours of practice? I may desire to leave a legacy, but to work consistently toward a single goal? Not this time around.

I keep one memento, though, as a reminder that passion is possible, even if for a brief period.

While living at St. Stephens Indian Mission in Wyoming, I visited blind Matilda, an elderly Arapaho whose face truly was lined in all the right places—laughter, sorrow, and pain. Often, she looked out on the dry hills as if a vision called to her. She would tilt her head and listen.

I wanted to draw her. Oh, how I wanted to draw her.

During a visit home, I came across a painting in *Arizona Highways* of a woman who looked a lot like Matilda. The work rendered the woman in velvety turquoise necklace and red dress, flowered kerchief and wrinkled skin—more Navaho than Arapaho.

"What medium would you use?" my mother asked.

Hoping my effort would avoid clutter and result in simplicity, I said, "Pen-and-ink."

"A difficult medium, Toni." She added. "Takes patience."

I didn't think to say, "For once I want something classier than the pinto pony."

We walked into the airy studio she and my brother-in-law had converted from the garage. The space belonged to my mother, who at age sixty-eight, had claimed a room of her own, filled with paints and paper. Around the room hung student art pieces done in watercolor, pen-and-ink, tempera, acrylic, and pencil: a seascape and lion at rest, lilies in a vase, a farmhouse peeking through the wheat. These pieces plus twenty others would be part of an annual exhibit at the local bank.

I sat at an easel that could have belonged to four-year-old Trina or eighty-year-old Dr. Brennan. In any case, on a summer morning, in my mother's studio, I had come to learn. She demonstrated the strokes I would need to create the drawing. For one full day and with inked pen, I experimented with lines and flicks, dots, and crisscrosses. My mother did not hover or compare pen-and-ink pieces with mine. She left me completely alone.

First, my woman would be rendered in pencil, a careful sketch of the head, eyebrows, nose, and sunken mouth. Gradually, her entire face, weathered by sun and lined with age, sprung from one-dimensional paper and pencil strokes. The eyes, though, vexed me. I wanted them blind but seeing, weary but alert. I stopped trying to force the eyes to emerge. Instead I let them sink deep, like dark pools. That was when I captured her shriveled, wise, wonderful face.

The hard work done, I began to trace over the pencil with pen and ink. Stroke by stroke she came alive beneath my hand: an old woman, a tribal face, and my own face years away. A self-portrait.

I completed the artwork one week later and far into the night. Early the next morning, I awoke, excited, and hurried into the studio. There, on the easel she gazed out. Her eyes held all I had hoped. I traced the crisscross lines around her mouth and chin. My fingers imagined the scarf's swirling texture and the coarseness of her hair and braid. Not a stroke too many. She was perfect. She was mine.

My mother entered the studio. She smiled. "Finished?"

"Finished."

She leaned close and paid me the greatest of compliments: "I wonder what she sees."

For years I kept the artwork in the living room so visitors would notice. "Toni, did you really do that?" Now, she has a place in my bedroom above my writing desk. Drawing—the desire going back to childhood that could have become a passion—never happened. She whispers to me what might have been.

"Rejoice in the good" continues to be a challenge. My better angels favor the idea of an equal playing field; my lesser angels suggest maybe I could occupy the higher ground. I glance sideways at those who overshadow me and wish I had nourished artistic, musical abilities. If I am honest, though, I admit that those who excel possess what I do not: a long-term commitment to accomplish the superlative. Why, then, would I bother to dress in denim and cowgirl hat and head for the carousel? Do I want to leap from horse to horse, trying to find the prettiest? Chances are that when the carousel shuddered to a halt, I would be hanging on to the pole for dear life, devastated that I never got to ride the chestnut stallion with the turquoise tassels.

Shun the World

That they not make inquiries into worldly affairs regarding things and business foreign to their calling, or losing time in frivolous talk.

To become a nun in the late 1950s and early 1960s meant to leave "the world." What would we find once we left? On the door leading into the Franciscan novitiate building was a sign that read "Enclosure. No Admittance." Our Lady of Angels Convent walled in a secret universe and excluded "seculars" from all but the main chapel and a parlor set aside for designated visits. No eating or drinking with seculars, no visiting their homes, and no conversation with seculars except "what is necessary and to the purpose."

Nevertheless, the outside world had a way of slipping in. To begin with, our main house had its worldly history. Originally built in the 1920s for the Hamilton Corbett family, the residence was an estate, set high in the lush hills of Southwest Portland. The Franciscan Sisters bought the eighteen-acre property in 1942: a three-story ivy-covered mansion with foyer and wide staircase, a library, polished oak floors, and a sunken living room. There were large windows to let in light, a parlor with attached kitchenette, and French doors leading out to a brick patio, rose gardens, and an orchard. Over the next decade, the sisters added a novitiate building, kitchen, dining rooms, gymnasium, and main chapel. Although the grounds were known as the Convent of Our Lady of Angels on Palatine Hill, we humble Franciscans were linked irrevocably with the famous Corbetts and their life of wealth.

Families from this exclusive Dunthorpe neighborhood celebrated Mass with us, prayed in the chapel, and sought counsel from the professed sisters. On sunny days, students from Lewis & Clark settled on blankets spread out on our sprawling lawn. In jeans and T-shirts, they ate lunch, laughed, and studied. None of the seculars, even the young, bright, and enthusiastic, however, stepped inside the novitiate door marked "Enclosure."

We may have lived a life unfamiliar to outsiders, a life devoid of jewelry, colorful fabric, and gilded mirrors, yet we Franciscans possessed a magnificent chapel. Bringing their worldly expertise, the designer, architect, and builder sat with the nuns and negotiated a contract. No expense sacrificed, the sisters imported from France life-size wooden carvings of St. Francis, the Sacred Heart, Virgin Mary, St. Joseph, and the massive crucified Jesus Christ suspended over the sanctuary. The fourteen Stations of the Cross fit against the chapel walls. Italian marble comprised those walls as well as the pillars and altar railing. Rows of eight-foot-high stained-glass windows glittered on both sides and stained glass blazed across the choir loft wall. "God's House deserves the best," Sister John Aloysius said.

Catholics believed that the White House deserved the best, too, and with the election of 1960, the political world began to filter into the convent. John Fitzgerald Kennedy, the sophisticated, articulate Commander in Chief, was our first Catholic president, of Irish descent, and a man of the world. The new first family brought Hyannis Port, the yacht, Brooks Brothers' suits, and Oleg Cassini fashions closer to us.

Catholic and Irish—what more could the Sisters of St. Francis at Our Lady of Angels Convent desire? The congregation had a formation house in Mallow, Ireland, which guaranteed that a large group of sisters with Irish roots journeyed from home to serve God in America. One of the Election Day stories related how a novice, in preparing the celebratory snickerdoodles, had accidently substituted chili powder for cinnamon. Sister Veronica Ann, in charge of the kitchen, let it be known, in her distinct brogue, that she suffered fools and mistakes in a similar manner. After the novice removed the cookies and placed them on the racks, she turned to offer Sister a sample. Sister Veronica Ann took one bite. Her dark eyebrows lifted to touch her forehead band and her ruddy cheeks blushed purple. But then, instead of anger at hundreds of cookies ruined, she laughed and said, "Red-hot cookies for a red-hot president." JFK, with Jackie on his arm, emanated a worldliness in which the nuns found no fault. To say he was "our president" contained a bit of a self-congratulation: the nuns believed that those in habit and clerical garb who cast their ballots had ushered John Fitzgerald Kennedy into the Oval Office.

The world continued to intrude, even in the enclosure. Although we young nuns did not read the secular newspapers, listen to the radio, or watch the nightly news, we had an effective substitute. For a half-hour every weekday evening, while we entertained ourselves at recreation, Sister John Aloysius joined the other professed sisters in the main house and watched Cronkite on CBS or Huntley and Brinkley on NBC. She shared the brief highlights—what she determined we needed to know—of Kennedy's debacle at the Bay of Pigs, the Cuban Missile crisis, the escalating conflict in Vietnam, Martin Luther King Jr. and the civil rights movement. Yet, true to the times, it was never meant for our round-table discussion or dinner conversation. Our task as postulants and novices was not to debate world affairs, but to keep them in our prayers.

"Don't mix politics with religion, and for goodness' sake, do not discuss either at the dinner table," my mother often said. No need to have conflicts upset polite conversation (a warning that my father did not heed). One of these areas of conflict centered on the Bible. While we Catholics could recite, by heart, the answers in *The Baltimore Catechism*, we were neophytes in our comprehension of the Holy Book. We were expected to leave all biblical interpretation to the priests who shaped our knowledge through the sermon at Sunday Mass. And open the Bible for personal prayer? Only heretical Protestants did that. Like most families, we Kennedys placed our

Bible in a conspicuous location where it could be seen and dusted, but never opened.

The unmentionable world of the Bible became a major topic of conversation in the convent. With regard to anything dealing with Scripture study, Sister Theona was a fearless proponent of opening doors to the outside. She introduced us to theologians who had taken up the challenge of Pope Pius XII in 1942: use the tools of the secular world to understand the Bible. Unlike the parish priest, Sister Theona introduced us to revolutionary thinkers like Pierre de Chardin, the French Jesuit paleontologist and geologist. Because of discoveries like the Dead Sea Scrolls, no longer was the Word of God to be taken literally, so no more strict interpretation of a six-day creation or a "real" Jonah inside the whale's belly. Sister taught us that the Bible is a combination of history, parable, metaphor, and myth. "Scripture is not in competition with science," Sister said. "The Bible does not tell us how the heavens go, but how to go to heaven."

She not only encouraged us to read and learn about the newest Scripture studies, but provided the place and resources. Downstairs, across from the novitiate library, was a gold mine of magazines. *The Bible Today, Crossroads, Commonweal, Christianity Today,* and *America* introduced us to a changing Catholic Church whose theological and scriptural view relied not only on tradition, but on history and literature and science.

Right in the midst of a study that fascinated and invigorated us nuns, came Vatican II, that splendid convocation of bishops meeting in Rome. The face of the renewal? A rotund, unassuming, gentle revolutionary named Pope John XXIII. "Throw open the windows of the church and let the fresh air of the spirit blow through," he said, and many Catholics were eager to do so. *Aggiornamento* was the watchword and "bringing-up-to-date" was its translation.

For those of us in religious life, the word meant a movement away from outmoded traditions and a return to our roots. For Franciscans that became an invitation to travel beyond our rigid nineteenth-century German foundation and back to the joy of thirteenth-century Francis of Assisi. Vatican documents encouraged us to discuss options for work, for dress, and for rituals. For all the Catholic faithful, bringing-up-to-date gave a radical definition to "secular." Instead of outsiders, or individuals on a lesser rung than priests and nuns, lay people were our partners. No more hierarchical model of the cleric, the married, and the single, but a community of God called together to be fearless leaders and servants, wily as serpents and gentle as doves.

The first concrete expression of *aggiornamento* struck at the heart of the Catholic tradition: the Holy Sacrifice of the Mass. From the first moment I toddled into a Catholic Church, I knew where the priest belonged: on the steps of the altar, his arms raised, his back to the congregation, and his words in Latin. We faced forward, like soldiers of Christ, armed with the cross of Jesus, following our priest-leader into the battle against evil.

When a new altar appeared at Our Lady of Angels, no longer was it out of reach, but set on the floor, at a level with the rest of us. At 6:30 in the morning, our dear Father

Harrington strode into the sanctuary, but this time he did not climb steps and turn his back on us. Instead, looking a little sleepy, and with a sheepish grin on his face, he stood at the new altar, spread his arms wide, and pronounced in English (not Latin): "The Lord be with you."

And the group of us responded in English (not Latin): "And with your spirit."

I smiled and thought, *So this is what Father looks like early in the morning.* He must have been thinking the same thing about us.

Aggiornamento. No longer a single marching line, but a community, the People of God, ushering our worship and rituals into the modern era.

Jubilation has a short life, but we believed that the dialogue between religion and the outside world would continue. In 1963, during the last two months of my canonical year, that first year as a novice, Pope John XXIII died of cancer, and a new Pope had taken his place. We believed that nothing, not even new leadership, could halt the momentum of Vatican II. Five months later, in November, John F. Kennedy was assassinated. When the announcement of the shooting came over the intercom, we novices closed our study books and sat stunned. His death followed soon after.

Sister John Aloysius rolled a bulky RCA television into the community room. As the grainy picture sputtered into focus, the room, usually buoyant with laughter, turned heavy with mourning. Our grief was communal, a heavy pall of disbelief and a smothering of hope. We watched Jackie, a veil blurring her face, and Caroline and John Jr. standing on

either side of their mother. We cried as John John saluted.
When the magnificent, fractious Black Jack trotted with an
empty saddle and boots placed backwards, we witnessed the
end of Camelot. We may have been protected nuns, but we
wept at the passing of John Fitzgerald Kennedy who had,
once upon a time, been our president.

The new year, 1964, brought beginnings and endings.
For those of us second-year novices, it would be our last
months in the novitiate. Before long we would leave the
enclosure. We would go out among seculars, worship with
them, and teach their children. As citizens, we would place
our trust in Lyndon Baines Johnson, an old hand at political intrigue, and as members of a religious order, we would
pledge obedience to Paul VI, a man fearful of what Vatican
II had unleashed. We would learn what it meant to be "in the
world, but not of it."

༒

On a day when Portland's clouds hung low over a tree-lined
walkway cutting north and south through Portland State's
sprawling campus, I met Jim, a friend who considers himself
blessed with financial security, family, and faith. That day,
though, melancholy added years to his face. "If I had known
what life had in store, I would have joined the Jesuits," he
said. "The world is too much."

The encounter with Jim brought to mind my past convent life. From entrance day in 1961 until final vows in 1970,
the Franciscan congregation established clear directives to
shield us from the worldly newspaper, radio, or television.

In many ways, however, I identified with that uncomplicated enclosure and did not want the negative to intrude. The straight, level, concrete walkway from convent to classroom and back again was a metaphor for how I could find peace away from the complexities of the world, the restlessness rising once more within me, and the yearning to be somewhere else. While some of the sisters with whom I lived proved to be politically engaged, I narrowed my focus to teaching primary children to read, grow lima beans, sing "Up with People," and dance to selections from the *Nutcracker Suite*. Weekday mornings we stood, placed our hand over our heart, and pledged allegiance to the flag—a traditional reminder to honor our veterans and the ideals of our nation. Where was I for the six years following first vows? Pretty much missing in action.

Talking with Jim revived religious community regulations and my own desires to stay ill-informed but relevant. No lingering, for me, upon Selma, inner city riots, Martin Luther King dead on a Memphis balcony, Bobby Kennedy dead in a Los Angeles kitchen, violence outside the halls of the Democratic Convention, or body bags coming home from war. Closer to home, though, I said farewell to the traditional habit and accepted, hesitantly at first, the shorter skirt and simple veil, the wave of hair and fashionable shoes, a garb in black and white, but oh, so much more modern. From among the secular on display I made my choices.

An initial awakening happened in the summer of 1970 when a sister colleague dragged me to a Vietnam War protest march that was to begin on the Marylhurst College campus and end at Lewis & Clark College. Figuring that the provincial, who would have nixed this participation, was in Zambia, I joined the protesters, but fear of getting caught dampened my enthusiasm. Trying to dodge a photographer, I sidled towards the peace posters. Once the line started moving, there he was, camera ready. Click. And what was the harmless little backdrop? In blazing red was a blood-spattered "Hell, No, We Won't Go." A vision of the newspaper landing on the provincial's desk was not a welcome one, but before long, the excitement of the protesters proved contagious.

We trekked along the highway, cheering for peace, clapping for justice, and waving to honking cars. Caught up in rebellion and a cause, we wound along the route through the Terwilliger neighborhood and into the Lewis & Clark chapel. Listening to speakers call for an end to deceit and an end to war, I wanted in on revolution and savored the role of dissident.

Years later, my friend Greg said it best: "Toni, Harriet Nelson put you to sleep, and Janis Joplin woke you up."

It was ironic that Jim regretted not joining the Jesuits. More than any religious order, the followers of St. Ignatius Loyola immerse themselves in the world. Their history is both heroic and flawed, but withdrawal has never been their calling. What would my life have been without Jesuits William Hayes, the poet Gerard Manley Hopkins, activist Daniel Berrigan, or the leader of Catholics today, the worldly-wise Pope Francis? Academics, missionaries, scholars, martyrs, and authors are the domain of Jesuits, who for some ill and much good, never hid behind walls.

Like Jim, though, the world can seem too much for me, and I imagine myself disappearing into a cherry tree or hidden in the closet with my flashlight and a pile of *Classics Illustrated*. On the way to a dental appointment, I rode east on Portland's MAX light rail and watched the twenty-first century up close. Against the "DO NOT WALK" sign, an old man pushed his cartload of belongings. Outside the Greyhound bus depot, a woman begged, aided by a pit bull and a baby. Tents and garbage—Portland's own riverside Hooverville—stretched under the Steel Bridge. I shut my eyes to block out the world.

When did I first view the world as out of my control? In 1978, the Catholic world awaited the election of a new Pope. Paul VI, who had alienated many not only by his fear of Vatican II, but by his official condemnation of artificial birth control, was dead. The laity saw a new beginning with Polish, not Italian, John Paul II. He would contribute youth, intelligence, and vibrancy to a bloated papal bureaucracy. If he could bend so nimbly on ski slopes, surely he would show similar resilience to a Church of opposing views. That was the hope.

Instead, he put into positions of authority those who cracked down on the American nuns, demanded they return to traditional convent settings and religious garb, and turn away from worldly pursuits. Even with the dire shortage of priests, he refused to discuss a married clergy or women's ordination. Most religious orders—except for the radical few—bowed to his word.

The secular world was just as disheartening to me. In the early 1980s, Ronald Reagan occupied the Oval Office. In his amiable way, Reagan took care of the wealthy and cut housing for the poor. He built up our nuclear arsenal. In the crosshairs of his desire to defeat Communism was Central America, land of wealthy clerics beholden to the military, ground of oppressed and tortured peasants, and country-side of the four missionary women—three nuns and one lay colleague—who were raped and murdered. I participated in protest marches in Portland and New York City, but the thousands of us who opposed policies had no effect on the world or the decisions of our leaders.

In a manner that proclaimed the marriage of politics and religion, Pope John Paul affirmed the fear of Ronald Reagan and chastised those who sought to end military dictatorships in Central America. A 1983 photo, taken on the tarmac in Nicaragua, still grieves me. Pope John Paul II in white robes stands over a kneeling Ernesto Cardenal. The Pope wags an angry finger close to Cardenal's upturned face. Both men are ordained priests. The man standing advocates for workers in his Polish homeland. The one kneeling seeks economic jus-tice for his fellow Nicaraguans. One is leader of the Catholic Church, the other is Minister of Culture for the Sandinis-tas, a revolutionary government. One is a fierce protector of traditional doctrine and the other a proponent of liberation theology.

The effect that this 1983 photo had upon me extends far beyond my resentment of a scolding Pope. Seeing Cardenal kneel was how I saw my own life under the dominance of a president and Pope, bedfellows, whose rigid policies seemed encased in concrete. I ached for Cardenal and Central America. I ached for the Church and for those of us in religious life. Religion and politics, never discussed at the dinner table, wielded unchecked power.

Of the three virtues of faith, hope, and love, the greatest is not love, but hope, that tiny bird of Emily Dickinson's.

> *"Hope" is the thing with feathers -*
> *That perches in the soul -*
> *And sings the tune without the words -*
> *And never stops - at all —*

In 2005, ugly reports of torture at Abu Ghraib and pedophile priests continued to surface. Both government and religious leaders lied and found black holes in which to annihilate critics and conceal crimes. Both reached for lawyers to plead their cause and justify their actions. On a morning when I sorely needed a birdsong thrumming in my soul, a walk through the neighborhood provided sunshine and clear air, ducks swimming in the wetland pond, and a romping labradoodle in the field. The homeowner's association had recently fixed the fountain and water burbled over stones. Neighbors waved on their way to work. It was a good day to be alive, a day for a breeze to rustle leaves to the ground.

That's when I saw it. Lying at the foot of a tree was a dead baby bird—transparent, but perfectly formed. One more dead bird shouldn't have mattered, but it did. That day, hope was not a thing with feathers, but a fragile, hollow-boned creature.

Eleven years later, in downtown Portland, I watched a new generation march for jobs, police accountability, racial equality, and an end to the plight of those who survive under bridges and inside shabby tents. They chanted: "No justice. No peace!" Drivers lost patience. Horns blared at these free spirits, who had slipped out from enclosures. Technology and an open society had linked them to a new world. A murder of noisy crows congregated on the Keller Auditorium roof, as if to hail them.

One part of me wanted to join the crowd; another said, *Pretty soon, they'll see it's useless.* Did I need to warn them to shun a world you cannot change? Maybe not. Maybe hope can perch precariously without falling. On an autumn afternoon, the few protesters multiplied into the many, and the many halted the traffic in a run-away world. They journeyed on an old route, trekking across slippery rocks, believing a perfect world is just a quick jaunt around a bend, and on up a hill.

Repose

You are here to kneel
Where prayer has been valid. And prayer is
more
Than an order of words . . .

T.S. Eliot, "Little Gidding"

Listen to the Silence

That they not forget so great is the importance of religious silence that on the strict observance of it depend, in a great measure, the progress made in the other virtues.

I grew up at a time when it was believed that a child should be seen and not heard. In classrooms I sat still while the teacher talked—one of forty youngsters kept under strict control. Golf demanded hours of sparse conversation and quiet courtesy. Our phone was a squat, durable invention with a rotary dial set aside for my mother's personal calls and my father's response to medical emergencies. Favorite places of play were the woods behind our house or high in the cherry tree, two magical rooms of solitude.

We were a family of readers, each of us children gobbling books whole. Reading's solitary nature kept the house quiet, but the stories thrust us toward mysterious islands and into spooky attics. Books contained a secret garden to tend and a crocodile to ride. A page-turner did not foster the meditative act, but jettisoned us into worlds where swords flashed and mutiny simmered. Externally, reading may have been the body's quiet occupation, but internally reading was the soul's wild romp.

If early childhood contained more outward silence than talk, the tranquil atmosphere changed once I turned twelve when we acquired a television. The prattle and hullabaloo of *I Love Lucy* along with the blazing guns and saloon talk of *Gunsmoke* disturbed the peace. At high volume, 45s and LP records of Elvis and Doris Day rang through the house. Golf's new attraction centered on the night thrill of whooping around in electric carts. Once Mary headed to college and Michael to the army, the phone and its extra-long cord belonged primarily to me. Earning a driver's license meant freedom: dragging Main Street; grabbing a hamburger and root beer at the A & W Drive-In; with boisterous girlfriends, picking up football players in town for the annual Shriner game.

Beneath the effusive extrovert, I still treasured quiet places much like the garden and the tree. There was silence in the unlocked St. Mary's Church, in the convent chapel at school that the sisters kept open for students, and in my bedroom. But then the phone rang, ball games needed cheering, Friday night dances swept me into fast motion. Escapes into tranquility vied with the socially-connected girl I felt compelled to be.

Silence had its dark side. Conflicts cast shadows, most of them emanating from my father. To hide his financial straits, my mother said, "It is in poor taste to discuss money." To shield my father's alcohol and drug abuse, we did not discuss the ever-present wine glass or the pills or "talk about family problems outside the home."

We moved to Pendleton in 1954, where my father was a physician and diagnostician in residence at the Eastern Oregon State Hospital. On too many Thursday afternoons, in anticipation of the silence to come, I would look out our living room window, and see not only the barred windows of the hospital, but the dark smoke arising from the crematorium. Before the cremains rested in ochre canisters, before the workers collected the ash, and before the furnace fires were lit, my father performed the autopsies, a task at which he excelled, a task in which he found no satisfaction. After work he would stride up the hill, come into the house without a word, go directly to the bedroom, and then to the bathroom. Soon, shower water ran, washing away the smell of intestine and bone. Those Thursday afternoons and evenings passed in a silence that comprised, for my father, more relief than rest.

What finally rendered him mute was not weariness or depression, but the stroke he suffered during my senior year. In our living room of tall windows, he consigned himself to a corner card table and a bulky reel-to-reel tape recorder. Day after day he leaned close to the microphone, spoke into it, replayed the halting phrases, and struggled with the verses again. How often from February to May did he falter, trying to twist his weary tongue around Tennyson's words?

Twilight and evening bell,
And after that the dark!

And may there be no sadness of farewell,
When I embark.

One day the recorder clicked off for good. My mother stored
the machine in the garage off the breezeway. No longer did
he hold his treasured poetry volumes. No longer could he sit
in his easy chair and recite by memory lines from "Song of
Hiawatha." To attempt clear phrases invited being pitied, so
my father ebbed into a man of fewer and fewer words. The
silence surrounding him was not dangerous, but terribly sad.

Convent stillness offered a different silence, a fundamental
element below the sounds. No matter which room I entered,
quiet filled the space like gossamer, in accordance with this
admonition: "Talking is altogether forbidden in the refectory,
dormitories, cells, and in the corridors of the house and the
workrooms." Add to this list: cloister walks, chapels, main
house, libraries, and station path. By coming to the convent,
I had reentered childhood, into a still realm that offered its
own rewards. I equated silence with peace and moral excellence. Even recreation in the community room was more of
a place of listening than speaking.

The art of a convent's quiet world required repetition.
I likened it to a golf swing—the muscle memory that accompanied stepping up to the ball—or given my penchant
for fashion, silence as a garment, like the lavender sweater
and matching plaid skirt I'd left hanging in my bedroom
closet. Each evening as we ended our recreation, a second-
year novice went to the bookshelf and picked up the small

bell. As soon as the ping sounded, we entered into Night Silence. Quietly we lined up and processed into little chapel for Compline, our evening prayer. From dawn to dusk, we abstained from talk because "great is the importance of religious silence."

Throughout the days and months, the convent novitiate kept its rhythmic flow, unbroken by talk. In the quiet I learned anew the art of courtesy and the attention required to set a pan down quietly, to keep my feet still against the library chair, and to shelve a book with care. Living among thirty others, we avoided "noise of any kind so as not to disturb any sister." More and more I liked the way stillness warmed, like tomato soup on a winter day.

Convent silence had its dark side as well, though the instances numbered few. Not talking is how the nuns kept secrets and discouraged curiosity. We did not say goodbye to the postulant or novice who "left." What stayed behind was the silent, empty chair at breakfast. Did we share our memories of her or pray for her at morning Mass? Not that I recall. Waking to hear a sister cry from a nightmare did not give anyone the right to comment the next morning. At times, the secrets unsettled me because they mirrored family sorrows gaining strength in the night.

Learning the value of silence coincided with the end of romance and adventure novels and the beginning of spiritual reading. This designated half-hour was not a race through a book, but a meditative walk through words, stopping along the way with the author to engage in an inner conversation and an opening of our minds to new wisdom. From the collection in the novitiate community room, we selected books to deepen our spiritual life. Gerald Vann's *The High Green Hill* was my first choice, initially not for its message, but its cover. Albrecht Durer's woodcut of intricate slits and gouges depicted a knight riding through a ravine of rocks, barren branches, and shattered debris. Serene, he passed Death and the Devil on his way to the mountain castle. After I feasted on the artwork, and was ready to read and relish Vann's insights, the chapters invited me to seek a commitment to Christ as missionary, to cast aside fear, to "launch into the deep," and to sacrifice my own comforts to heal others. Most importantly spiritual reading meant going back to savor sentences and paragraphs, a way of treating a book differently from my childhood experience. Instead of inhaling a novel, spiritual reading taught me the art of the slow act; to take all the time I needed to let insights settle in my mind and heart.

Meditation brought an even deeper quiet. Sister John Aloysius told us how Francis of Assisi would slip off into hillside caves where he could look out on a panorama of crag and tilled fields, green grass and sky. In these places of solitude, Francis felt closest to God. I had no cave in which to escape, but main chapel was the perfect spot for meditation with its deep-set stained-glass windows, sweeping arc of Communion rail, and the open arms of the crucified Christ suspended over the sanctuary. In contrast to my ambivalent relationship with community, prayer eased my tension. Even though I was surrounded by others, I felt like a young mystic wrapped in and soothed by stillness. Each month in her small, ordered office, Sister John Aloysius folded her hands on the desk, leaned slightly forward, and watched me, her brown eyes demanding truth.

"Antoinette, how is your prayer life proceeding?"

Without hesitation, I would answer, "Well, Sister."

Outside chapel, in the rush of charges and responsibilities, I had to labor to stay in God's presence. A simple prayer called me inward—a prayer that occurred whenever a clock chimed. One place in particular was the cool, subdued space of the novitiate library, where I read *The Summa Theologica*— Aquinas' proof of God's existence. The library clock began to chime.

A sister said, "Let us remember the Holy Presence of God."

We answered, "Let us adore His Divine Majesty."

At that point I set aside pen and followed the familiar ritual: closing my eyes, I listened as the bells rang out the hour. Fluorescent lights snapped and rain slapped the library window and I slipped under the sounds. When the chimes finished, I picked up the pen and returned to Aquinas and his lengthy, labored arguments on behalf of God.

Of all the silent times that first year, my favorite occurred during Holy Week, the days leading up to Easter Sunday. After evening Mass on Holy Thursday, the community began Good Friday's vigil. The altar and sanctuary were stripped bare—no cloth, flowers, or candles—except for the monstrance that radiated light like a gold sunburst. When the chimes signaled eleven o'clock, a companion and

I moved forward and genuflected beside the prie-dieu. The nuns kneeling there stood and we took their place. The ritual honored Jesus, grieving and lonely, who asked his sleeping disciples in the Garden of Gethsemane, "Could you not watch one hour with me?" I entered into the Presence of God as a disciple in the Garden. When the chimes rang out twelve strokes, serge rustled nearby. My companion and I stood. The next two nuns took our place.

Outside chapel, the cool air brushed against my face. I moved down the cloister walk, through the enclosure, and into the dormitory. I pulled aside a curtain slightly and tapped the metal railing at the foot of a bed. The sleeping nun stirred, ready for her turn to watch. I entered my own cell, knowing that hour after hour the ritual would continue, all the way through to dawn of Good Friday. I fell asleep, surrounded and comforted by silence.

From 2011 until 2017, I lived in downtown Portland, first in an apartment and then in a condo. At first I thrived. Views of the cityscape, the proximity of museums, the theater, symphony, and coffee shops seemed a sophisticated and compelling landscape. The trolley, MAX, or my feet brought freedom from the car and satisfaction with my minimal carbon footprint. My eighth-floor condo view looked south to the tree-covered hills and east to snow-capped Mt. Hood. A sunrise glowing lavender to magenta could take my breath away.

Then the desire to live forever in that place disappeared. I longed to step outside onto solid ground, rather than endure the confinement of elevator and stairwell. Bus and trolley, car and MAX noise rattled my peace, the city's dirt and litter cluttered my soul, and the expense of downtown living pricked at the nun in me. And all the cultural events I had planned on attending? I could count easily my visits to museums or attendance at the symphony, ballet, or theater. And when did a coffee shop offer a richer cup than the foamed mocha I concocted myself? I longed for lush green places and quiet.

Outside the city now, I find both silence and green. My dwelling is not Palatine Hill, with cloister walks and a station path winding through the woods. The downtown sunrise no longer paints the morning sky. Yet outside my window, a maple grows. I cannot climb it or hide among the leaves as I did in childhood. But the tree offers respite. In autumn, my favorite season, I watch the leaves turn color without making a sound.

Friends ask what I miss most about the convent. Without a doubt, the time allotted for silence—regulated times of quiet as essential as eating, sleeping, and working. People will argue that I can do that outside of the cloister. Not always true, and certainly not that simple. Unless I am careful, I relegate silence to a far-off corner, waiting until I am less fragmented and have the leisure for it. But all too soon, the day is done, gone the sun, and gone the opportunity.

As a high school student, I had shivered with dread reading Margaret Ann Hubbard's *Murder Takes the Veil*, deliciously terrorized by the bulky nun stalking a college campus. *The Nun's Story* by Kathryn Hulme described Sister Luke as stifled by the brooding quiet. But the writing that bests captures the mystery of convent quiet is Mark Salzman's slender gem, *Lying Awake*. Salzman creates a contemplative world where silence is a gateway into ecstasy and understanding. I have never experienced, as Salzman's protagonist has, either the barrenness of God's absence or the iridescence of His glory, but I, too, have experienced a quiet that permeates and heals both the natural world and spaces of the heart.

I cling to the best of my past. At bedtime, I tuck the computer in the closet and leave the iPhone on the dining room bookshelf. I drop the bedroom blinds, pull the curtains, and read in my chair while Angel digs deep, like her wolf ancestors, into the dog cushion. Gradually both of us settle into the quiet befitting a sleeping canine and her fragmented guardian. Some nights, before I climb into bed, I light a candle and say evening prayer aloud. If I am restless, I place the rosary on the pillow, confident that once I slip under the covers, the beads and repetition will help me sleep. Before I turn off the light, I go to my desk, where, beneath the pen-and-ink Navaho woman, sits a brass elephant bell. I lift it from its cradle, ring it once, and whisper, "Let us remember the Holy Presence of God. Let us adore His Divine Majesty."

Blend In

That they dedicate themselves entirely to works of charity toward others, in order, thereby, to attain perfection; for the bond of perfection is charity.

When my father slammed the front door and gunned the car away from our house, my mother did not complain about him. Instead she worked in the kitchen, slicing apples for pie or mixing cookie dough. She washed counters and cleaned out drawers, and all the while she hummed. Sometimes she sat at the Chickering upright and played, her calm belying her inability to understand her husband. Often she sang while ironing or folding clothes, but her voice treaded softly, in a strained soprano, as if afraid to break free.

My father often disappeared into music as well. Why, all those times, did the phonograph play Irish tenor John Mc-Cormick, the songs forcing a frown, or slight tremble around my father's mouth? Maybe "Mother Machree" made him long for his own mother, who died too early. Maybe "When You and I Were Young, Maggie" recalled promises he made to my mother. "It's a Long Way to Tipperary," might have been regret for his refusal to take the research position at Mayo Clinic (my mother hated the cold). And the fiddle of "The Kerry Dance" could have transported him to the Ireland of his father, the Ring of Kerry he longed to visit, and the castle he expected to claim. Melody made a melancholy promise that maybe someday he would discover where he belonged.

Woven in among the lovely liturgical songs and the harmony we nuns made while peeling potatoes and snapping beans was a reminder of my home—the shifting, unpredictable land of beautiful music and sadness. In the main chapel, seventy sisters bowed, sat, stood, genuflected, and knelt in unison. Then we sang. High notes hung in a single sweet tone and spun off the wide marble pillars and into the sanctuary. The nun, three pews behind me, hit the high notes with ease. A second-year novice, Sister was a lyric soprano with perfect pitch. She winced to hear notes off-key. When stressed, she hummed. Her face, long and slender, would have been beautiful if not for the lazy eye that made her appear distracted. Her smile strained her jawbone. Her laugh erupted, too brittle to be believed. She was the skinny doll I made from pipe cleaners, twisting the pieces tight to keep them in place. One day she said, "Antoinette, you remind me of myself," and I was afraid she might be right. I would be in community, but like my father, never quite fitting, wincing at missed notes.

As time passed, though, I discovered music in the novitiate bore little resemblance to my family experience. Music

did not exist for the individual's escape or diversion from
hurt, but began and ended in a deep belief that life was to be
celebrated together, an outward sign of our commitment to
the common good. Given that community stretched limited
human beings toward the ideal, harmony made that effort an
easier task. Melody gave to us nuns joy as well as a promise:
if we sang together we would stay together.

Unity found its metaphor in the official prayer of religious orders called the Divine Office. In the morning we recited psalms of Matins, Lauds, Prime, Terce, Sext, and None;
in late afternoon we prayed Vespers; at night we wished one
another safe sleep through the psalms of Compline. Some
religious communities sang or chanted the psalms. Our
Franciscan order did not, but the antiphonal nature of the
Divine Office was melodic and uniting as sisters on one side
of the chapel summoned all people to sing God's praise. Sisters across the aisle pledged to do that.

> *Sing praise to God, you faithful people.*
> *Remember what God has done*
> *and give thanks.*
>
> *So I will not be silent; I will sing praise to you.*
> *O God, you are my God;*
> *I will give thanks to you forever.*

Back and forth in question and answer, plea and promise the voices blended. As the Rule demanded, no one voice
prayed louder than the next. Rather we strived to be one

heart and one voice. We had these words of love and kindness to remember in times of impatience or irritation.

Gregorian chant melded easily with the Divine Office, but our teacher seemed a strange choice. Old, skinny, and bushy-browed, Sister Hilaria (who despite her name, rarely smiled) squeaked out how to sing light on high notes, mellow on low notes, and completely in unison. The first chant I remember singing was "Ubi Caritas": where love and harmony live, there is God. Not every sister sang in perfect pitch, but every sister sang the words of unity. We were to be notes on the *Missa*, scaling the demands of community one harmonic step at a time, and creating a composition held together by respect and love.

First attempts at convent belonging had made me feel like odd girl out. My set did not seek to escape life in the way I did, but met it with equanimity. In addition, four of them knew one another from high school. They accepted me as part of the group, but I had a difficult time accepting myself in that role. One gift, though, came to unite us. We could sing, and our signature melody was a love song from Handel.

Where'er you walk
Cool gales shall fan the glade.
Trees where you sit
Shall crowd into a shade.

The six of us sang in three-part harmony words that blended the wooded glen, a perfect love, and transformation. With each step the loved one takes, the breeze blows gently, and the trees form a circle of protection. When I recall our singing together, no one location stands out. We sang often, and the places blend one into another: the novitiate community room when feast day candles blazed on a cake; the foyer of the main house; the professed community room with its scarlet Oriental rugs and open fireplace; under a plum tree on visiting day. Strange how I forgot my differences when we blended one lilting phrase into another.

The novitiate years began to diffuse the familiar scene of watching my father listen to his favorite, often mournful songs. No more did I walk hesitantly into the living room, hear the notes, and determine the mood. Instrumentals played during recreation were joyful. Mozart and Debussy, Copeland and Vivaldi quickened the heart, the stitch, the conversation, as the puzzle pieces clicked into each other.

One day in our music appreciation class, our professor introduced us to Smetana's symphonic poem, The Moldau. The flute played, the strings sang, and together we nuns became the river, rippling over stones, gurgling close to river banks, through woodlands and meadows, passing by a wedding celebration and a moonlight folk dance. From Bohemia through Prague, we, with the river, accumulated, merged with the Elbe, and emptied triumphantly into the North Sea. Music that day, may have been an escape, but it was also a communal adventure.

Although my homesickness allowed me to paint a Norman Rockwell Christmas with my family, there was little truth in that image. We did have a decorated tree and presents beneath. We listened to carols and to Ebenezer Scrooge scratching out numbers, Marley's chains clanking, and Tiny Tim's "God bless us, every one," but the holidays were, for me, inevitably tinged with dread. Will my father drink too much? What will make him angry this time? My last family Christmas took place in the hospital, accompanied by the odor of Pine-Sol and the blare of intercom announcements.

My first Christmas in the novitiate taught me that Christmas could be a time, not of fear and disappointment, but hope and surprise. No gifts under the tree with colorful name tags, but that didn't matter, because the convent holidays were a feast for the senses: evergreen trees in the chapels and community rooms, wreaths and swags on the doors, candles burning on altars and tables, and cinnamon in the snickerdoodles, sticky buns, and apple pie. Color splashed in ribbons, ornaments, and poinsettias. "The Holly and the Ivy," "Lo, How a Rose E're Blooming," and "When Blossoms Flowered Mid the Snows" soared in three-part harmony. No anxiety, but an expectancy of something wonderful waiting, right around the corner.

The novices promised us postulants that the best was yet to come.

As we sat in the darkened community room on Christmas night, one by one candles appeared, flickering on the book shelves. Christmas tree lights and flames in the fireplace left an aura around a smiling Sister John Aloysius, and her dimples, always a surprise, appeared. Voices hushed, the phonograph played, and Dylan Thomas recited his poem, *A Child's*

Christmas in Wales, his husky, resonant voice remembering Christmases rolling "down toward the two-tongued sea like a cold and headlong moon." There were cats and a fire, fussy aunts and sleepy uncles, sherry and walnuts, presents both useful (scarves and socks) and useless (tin soldiers and jellied candies). The best lines, though, Thomas spoke at the end.

> *Always on Christmas night there was music . . .*
> *Looking through my bedroom window, out into the*
> *moonlight and the unending smoke-colored snow, I*
> *could see the lights in the windows of all the other*
> *houses on the hill and hear the music rising . . .*

"There's still more," the novices told us. "Christmas lasts until Epiphany." To honor the coming of the Magi, we gathered once again in the darkened community room amid flickering, colored Christmas lights. The novices laughed with Sister John Aloysius, and then turned to us, smiling, as if a joke were coming and soon even we postulants would recognize the punch line. Sister's graceful hands pulled the record from its jacket, placed it on the phonograph, and smiled, dimples softening her face. The music began, a slow, melodic opening of strings that fell into bass tones and then sprung to life with the woodwind, perhaps an oboe, followed by the soprano's call.

"*Amahl!*"

The boy tenor answered, *"Coming!"*

With my sisters, I entered the melodic story of the crippled boy who tells tall tales, whose mother cannot believe

that on this night, there is a sky so glorious, a sky shined by
damp clouds and swept clean by soft winds:

> *As if to make it ready for a King's ball.*
> *All its lanterns are lit,*
> *All its torches are burning.*

What would my first Christmas have been like without
Menotti's opera *Amahl and the Night Visitors?* Three tired
Kings, having traveled so far, seek respite with a poor widow
and her crippled child, but there is little sleep for any of
them. Instead, there are dancing shepherds, a banquet of
apples and raisins, walnuts and pomegranates, figs and cu-
cumbers, an attempted theft, a miracle, and a journey toward
a star, Amahl sings, "as large as a window."

Sister John Aloysius, her face radiant, mouthed the
words. *Amahl is her favorite part of Christmas,* I thought. That
night, another kernel of love appeared: appreciation for the
present instead of mourning for the past. Melody was an
escape into other worlds, but better yet, a communal ritual
of welcome.

For three years of my novitiate, always there was music.
It gathered and strengthened the bond among us in rooms
where we pared potatoes, knelt in prayer, or crocheted baby
booties; in moods where we felt weariness, joy, or irritation. For brief, keen moments, melody of poetry and psalm
united us, and we entered into the good that comes when
we no longer "make known the defects of others, or belittle
the good they do." Music freed me from my own conflicted, unloving self by leading me deep into the mystery of

community rituals. Music kept me coming back to my sisters, one day at a time.

After browsing in Powell's book store one day, I headed outside to witness a scene far from harmonious. On the corner of NW 10th and Burnside stood a long-haired, disheveled young man, his guitar slung across him, his open case speckled with coins, and his face flushed with anger. A few feet away, a woman squinted at him from a shabby brown blanket on the sidewalk. An empty coffee cup in front of her held spare change. Both had the wiry bodies and weathered faces of those who spend days, and perhaps nights, outside. He yelled for her to "get her own corner," and she yelled back that it was a free country. He played a riff. "At least I work for a living." All the while, pedestrians cut a wide swath around them while the bus and cars whizzed by.

The YouTube clip of the London Food Hall would have been a blessing here. Shoppers, intent on the task at hand, check out the onion and potatoes, the fish and cheese. All at once, one of the clerks—a tenor—begins to sing. A soprano joins, and a contralto. The store reverberates with "Funiculi, Funicula." Harmony pulls the shoppers out of isolation and into a community—smiling, capturing the music on an iPhone, and humming along.

What would have happened if the competing twosome on 10th Avenue had joined in song—the young man strumming, the woman adding her mezzo in harmony? If they'd chosen the chorus of Don McLean's "American Pie," or Adele's "Rolling in the Deep," would pedestrians have stopped to smile, snap photos, sing along, and toss in a coin or two? Maybe the driver of the trolley that stopped was a tenor with the Portland Opera. The whole delightful sequence could have gone viral. For a while, a happy alternative to angry outbursts on a city corner.

The sister with the pure soprano voice and anxious manner left the Franciscans after her first profession. Wherever she is, I hope she still sings. No longer do I fear her words, "You remind me of myself." Her love for music and struggles with community are mine as well, for kinship, whether claimed or not, is part of the human condition. Suffering and scarcity prowl my soul's sidewalks and the corner near Powell's. Yet I hold to an old belief: melody can help lift us, for a while, in unison.

That belief is kept alive by gentle reminders. One is a photograph of the six of us postulants in our black dresses, black capes, and white-trimmed black veils. Carol, Connie, Patricia, Kathleen, and I stand around the piano; Loretta sits at the baby grand, ready to play a duet with a novice beside her, while another novice balances a cello between her knees, her bow poised. Each time I look at the photo, I hear the introductory chords and the opening harmony of sisters linked together in song. And other reminders? Each Christmas I open my battered copy of Dylan Thomas' *A Child's Christmas in Wales*. Each New Year's Eve, I listen to *Amahl and the Night Visitors* in a living room lit with tree and candles. Music and mutual charity—often an easy mingling.

Other times, though, love presents a harsher challenge, like the evening in November of 2016, when I stood in the kitchen, furious after a black, miserable week. The presidential election had knocked the wind out of me. In addition, I had been substitute teaching for a week, explaining the difference between a diary entry and an essay and monitoring iPad use in study hall. Friends were coming for dinner, there was a table to set, a pile of dishes to wash, and veggies to cut. Cooking, which should have been a leisure activity, made my head hurt. Elizabeth Bishop's "Sonnet" rose unbidden—the speaker's need for music to turn bitter words into sweet, to invite melody to fall like raindrops, a soothing, calming inundation. Even though I spoke the melodic words aloud, they weren't enough. Needing real music, I played Alison Krause's CD "Down to the River to Pray."

Lifting the table cloth, I let it float over the table, like an altar cloth, like a baptismal gown. "Let's go down," I sang, lining up the forks and spoons, a silver community of mothers and fathers, sisters and brothers. Water ran hot, soap bubbles rose, and as I washed dishes, Krause and I sang, "Come on down" to the river's edge, where we will dip our feet, extend our hands heavenward, and pray for healing. I dried my hands and spun the towel. I pulled out the cutting board and knife, the bowl of peppers, carrots, onion, and broccoli, all the while singing, "Who shall wear the starry crown?" *Music*, I thought, *works every time*. Taking the knife and onion in hand, I peeled off the outer layer, and began to slice.

Live the Questions

That the superiors exercise great solicitude in the spiritual training of the Novices, and prefer this to their progress in study or work.

On a November day in 1954, I was in Pendleton, Oregon, a strange town, starting in a strange school called St. Joseph's Academy. The night before, I had put the book with math problems on the dining room table. My father, so smart, said, "We'll get these finished in no time." But we didn't, and I cried. I wanted to be back in Eugene and back in fifth grade with pretty Sister Stella Maris, who let us write stories and make a diorama of the Blessed Virgin.

My new teacher didn't smile and she wasn't pretty. Short and squat, she smelled like Listerine and her habit, like mothballs. I bent my head low over my paper, but she called on me anyway.

"Toni Kennedy?"

I stood, afraid and embarrassed. In front of new classmates, I answered, "Sister, I did not finish my homework."

She wrote my name in cursive on the upper right-hand corner of the blackboard, and all day long that is where the name stayed.

That night I knelt beside the bed. If I could have told my mother how much I hated school, would she and my father confront Sister? Never. They would not take my side against a teacher. Sister was always right. I begged God to make her disappear, so that tomorrow the principal would announce, "Poor Sister has gone to God." Together with my classmates I would fold my hands and bow my head in prayer, but my heart would leap sky-high.

God did not listen. One day followed the next. Sister, all powerful, made us stand and declare whether homework was finished or not, and she continued to write names on the blackboard. Never again did my name go up, but I found a way out of that classroom.

During Christmas vacation my father took the four of us children skiing on a slope in the Meacham Pass whose drifts piled high and harmless, perfect for the uninitiated. The air tingled my skin and the skis let me slither and slide down froth-white hills, nature cutting out thoughts of a walled-in classroom.

High above me, Michael and Alan shouted and whooped as they sped down, down. *My turn*, I thought. Trudging up the slope, I set my jaw, ready for a last spin to the bottom. One good shove and I was on my way, moving fast, but just before I met a little bump, my left knee locked in place, and when I hit the rise in the ground, I fell. Tangled in skis, aware of the pain, jarred by the ice-hot snow against my cheek, I cried out for my father. He carried me to the car, and drove too fast through the slippery mountain pass until we came into Pendleton and into the emergency room of St. Anthony's Hospital. A torn cartilage equaled crutches. Through January and part of February, I suffered pain real and imagined, and as if I had planned it, I missed school.

On the day I was to return, cast-free, I woke with a burning, itching rash around my waist. My father took one look and said, "Good Lord, Marjorie, how can someone her age get shingles?" For the next three weeks, I was allowed to stay home.

Once the shingles healed, I had to go back to Sister's classroom. I set the next day's clothes over the chair, and climbed into bed, but tossed and turned until early morning. By the time I was showered and dressed, my stomach churned so badly I could not eat. My father left for work at the State Hospital and my mother drove Mary, Mike, and Alan to school, but upon her return, she sat with me and said, "I know it's late, but I want you to try to go to school today."

With books in tow and my fingers scrunching the lunch sack, I huddled in the car. We passed St. Mary's Church and drove across the overpass. As soon as my mother took a left and parked in front of the brick Academy, I began to cry.

"Toni, what is it?"

"I can't go in."

She patted my hand, started the car, and we headed home. In the warmth of the kitchen, I took out the lunch, and thus, at ten o'clock in the morning, my mother and I shared the tuna and celery sandwich, potato chips, carrots, and peanut butter cookies. My stomach felt fine.

My parents did not speak about my attending school again, and I loved them for that with all my heart. I put the next months to good use. I read Nancy Drew and Hardy Boys mysteries. I ate Wheat Thins and slept late. In the summer, I walked back into the classroom with a substitute teacher and filled in worksheets to make up the six months I had missed, but never grasped either percentages or ratios. I had learned, though, a fact that I wrapped as tight as any of my father's secrets: if I do not have the answers, the classroom is a trap.

I endured seventh and eighth grades bluffing my way through studies. It wasn't all that difficult to do. At the dinner table, my father quizzed us on historical persons, literary characters, and sports stars (Floyd Patterson, Johnny Unitas, and any athlete from Notre Dame). I memorized the facts for safekeeping. Poetry volumes and his record collection gave me an introduction to Wordsworth, *Othello*, and *La Bohéme*. I watched *The $64,000 Question* game show and thanks to *Classics Illustrated* recognized storylines from Cervantes and Dickens to Twain and Verne. I continued, however, in the role of a struggling, mediocre math student.

Previously, St. Joseph's Academy maintained a strong curriculum and prestigious reputation in Pendleton, but by my senior year, a few nuns and one coach carried the brunt of science, history, English, typing, and math classes. My boyfriend and I, along with our aging, fearful Latin teacher, helped Hannibal cross the Alps. A dwindling student population and financial problems made inevitable the school's closure, but before that occurred, I graduated with my class—all fourteen of us.

After years of sly escape, I suffered an academic shock when I entered the convent. The other five postulants had come from two high-powered all-girls, college preparatory institutions. Diligent and focused, they were already students, and I was playing catch-up. I sat at attention in a wooden desk, feet set firmly on the green linoleum, notebook opened, head bent over a book, and pen poised. Like the early days in sixth grade, my first semester was a harsh experience. I tried not to be afraid.

Young, tawny-skinned, Italian, with sleepy brown eyes, Sister Eleanor Christine taught trigonometry. Trig. I had barely eked out a B- in geometry, but Sister was kind and I wanted to please her. One day she said to us, "Think about a new idea, a math question you haven't considered before. See if you can supply an answer." I began with the Pythagorean Theorem—a familiar concept—and I imagined artwork that would dazzle her. I memorized the definition, sure that behind square, side, angle, and hypotenuse, a new idea would arise.

After hours in the library, surrounded by red *World Book* and brown *Britannica* encyclopedias, I gained one valuable insight. All the implications of what Pythagoras studied and presented had been proved already. Humiliated, feeling small enough to fit in the dunce corner, I handed in an unfinished project.

Math trapped me again, but this time in music theory class. Sister Rosella, a brilliant Greek and Latin scholar as well as a gifted pianist and harpist, taught notation through number theory. No way could I connect chords with 1 and 4, or tonic and root notes. Sure that the others possessed the answers, I was ashamed to ask questions. Sister assigned us a piano composition project, one that we had to memorize. In my head, I composed a complex song—devoid of the number theory—with too many chords. On recital day, I volunteered first, terrified of what I'd forget. Hands poised, I began well enough, but then froze, unable to recall the composition. I improvised, bungling my way through a miserable two minutes.

The professor said gently, "That's enough, Antoinette. Return to your seat."

I felt the classroom close in. No exit in sight. Listening to the other compositions, simple and precise, I fretted that I hadn't attempted the same.

History was taught in the classroom where we had math and music theory, but in no way was I cornered. Instead, this professor's classes were a river of fresh water. All I had to do was dip my pitcher and fill it to the brim with clear, cool liquid. Sister Ethelwina, all five feet and ninety pounds of her, presented—amazingly—the grand sweep of Western culture's roots. Before the invention of PowerPoint or iPad, she could fascinate an audience because she detailed the stories behind a Pepin the Short or St. Patrick's fictional snakefest. With a shrug of one shoulder and a slight smile on her ascetic features, she lectured and I took notes. And my note paper? A messy jamming of the first few letters of unfamiliar persons, places, and things, and spaces galore to fill in later when I prowled the library for information. I loved filling the pitcher. And after her classes and all the research, I felt deliciously smart.

But it was Sister Theona, who taught English and theology who was my *alma mater*, mother of my soul. One day, Sister wrote three words on the blackboard: "Live the questions." And after the quotation, the name Rainer Maria Rilke. Stunned, I wrote the words down in my notes, and a door opened. Sixth grade taught me that answers showed how smart a student was. But the words on the board insisted on a different moral. It was the questions, and I had so many. I imagined myself in the midst of books, open and waiting. No papers to write, no performances to give, only knowledge to absorb. In Sister Theona's class, I stopped being afraid.

During first semester of my canonical year, three Holy Names nuns from Marylhurst, the women's college to which our Palatine Hill school was an affiliate, sat in the back. They had come to evaluate Sister Theona, part of an accreditation process every four years. Sister entered the classroom, her face ruddy, eyes bright, and her celluloid collar a bit askew. She had in her hand what I had never seen before in her classes—colored chalk. Sister Theona did not walk to the edge of the raised dais, nor did she open her hands in her characteristic gesture. Instead, she stayed close to the blackboard. Her upper lip caught on her teeth. Her left hand trembled. It brought back my

sixth-grade year, a Pythagoras project, and a music composition. Sister Theona was afraid.

That day, we protected her. If she asked us to compare
Mark's Gospel story of the blind man with that of John's, we
did it. If Jeremiah was a reluctant messenger, then we supplied an Isaiah in contrast. And Sister Theona recorded our
responses in red, green, and blue colored chalk. The Holy
Names nuns, those who sat in the back with their notepads
and evaluation sheets, smiled and nodded, and they would
leave to write sterling comments about the middle-aged,
plump little Franciscan who was scholar and teacher all the
way to her sturdy, black shoes.

I left the class, though, dismayed with the reversal I had
witnessed: bold students and a frightened educator. That day
I understood, a little, about the dangers of the intellect—not
only could it turn a person arrogant and domineering, but
could render a person small and shaking. There was no fun
or joy watching Sister Theona squirm.

As a young nun, who often felt overwhelmed by academics, I learned how the intellectual life, for all its possibilities,
could morph into a more treacherous place, a darkened room
with a wooden chair and an overhanging bright light—perfect for an interrogation.

To celebrate her seventy-eighth birthday, my sister Mary and
I enjoyed sweet rolls at Panera. The conversation led, as it often did, to our parents. Although our mother and father had
grown old together in relative peace and companionship, we

had not witnessed those qualities growing up in the Kennedy household. Mary, Michael, Alan, and I had tried to figure out their complicated relationship and its effect on us. As years passed, we felt amazement that the two of them had stayed together and gratitude for the unique inner life they had given us. A troubled combination of generosity and impracticality, of hope and disillusion, our parents immersed us in both chaos and creativity. We joked that they should have been born in some other century, with wealth and security as inheritance.

I shared with Mary the fact that I was grappling with this chapter on the intellectual life. "I'm missing a connection." I told her. "Did mom or dad push us to excel academically?"

She shook her head. "They didn't do that."

"I hated school."

"I was bored."

"I learned more with mom and dad than I ever learned in the classroom."

"Books and music and art." Mary smiled. "Multi-layered."

I liked that word and tucked it away for later.

Mary and I returned to the present. We discussed politics and religion—remnants of childhood. We laughed about *Fargo* and *Big Love*. We talked books: *Hillbilly Elegy* for me and Braun's *Cat* series for Mary—a gentle, audio diversion while she crochets blankets for Warm Up America! A good morning for us—like the old days.

Later, I opened my notebook to Rilke's quotation:

Have patience with everything unresolved in your heart and try to love the questions themselves, like locked rooms or like books written in a very foreign language. Live the questions now. Perhaps, then someday in the future, you will gradually, without even noticing it, live your way into the answer.

I read the words again. Questions can redeem the mind and the intellectual life.

In 1971, seventeen years after sitting terrified in her classroom, I lived in Franciscan community with that feared sixth-grade teacher. She was still squat, still gruff, but she didn't scare me. She was my sister, the one with the slow smile who had found her niche, not in math classes for elementary school children, but teaching art to high school students. The first time I entered her classroom, she sat, surrounded by long-haired boys, dressed in jeans and flannel shirts. A mix of football players and guys who drove pickups with gun racks might have been apt descriptions, but what most had in common was a keen dislike for school and failure in the classroom.

Nuns I lived with accepted that these "losers" were Sister's "winners." Young Jackson Pollocks in the making found a haven with Sister in her cluttered art room. She tacked their creations to walls and fastened others securely across the blackboard. Not a single inch available to shame students by writing their names in cursive. What makes a person a tyrant in one place and a facilitator in another?

In 1995 I spent a week with two friends at Manzanita, on the Oregon Coast. Hidden on one side by Douglas fir and blackberry bushes, our cabin sat high, and windows offered a wide ocean view. Early morning I opened the sliding glass doors and stepped out on the wooden deck. Far below, the beach was silent, free from joggers and canine retrievers.

A cat, earth-toned, peered at me from below the deck. At first glance, she seemed a kitten, but as she nuzzled the railing worn silken by rain, her tits dragged low. Her tummy rippled, like marbles in a velvet pouch. When I brought out coffee and pastry, she watched, and her tongue swept the edges of her mouth. I stood. She disappeared. I put a plate of tuna and a bowl of milk on the deck and left. She licked them clean and I refilled them. That evening she'd returned, crouched low, suspicious, but she lapped milk and gobbled tuna.

One friend said, "Careful, she's wild."

The next day, I moved the food containers close to the patio doors. She ate, curled into a circle, and slept. Later that day, I moved the food inside and left the door open. For two days, I let her come and go. At first, she ate quickly and disappeared, but as the week progressed, she stayed a little longer. She explored the bathroom, the bedroom, and the wood pile beside the stove. She settled inside.

"See," I said, "She likes it here."

"Toni, you know nothing about cats," one friend said.

"Leave her free to come and go," my other friend warned.

"Never fear," I told them. "I know what I'm doing."

My companions left for the afternoon, and I was alone with the cat. The door was wide open, and she slept on a cushion near the sofa. I took a look at her asleep, stood as quietly as possible, and pulled the doors shut.

Immediately awake and terrified, the cat hurled herself and her small living luggage from window to window, clawing the glass as she would a tree. She slid down, and climbed again. I tried to reach the door, but she flew in a frenzy, her body thumping against glass. Panic shot through me: *She will break her neck and it's my fault.* Crawling on my stomach over to the glass door, I pushed it open and covered my head. In one swift leap, the cat escaped, her soft belly brushing my hands, and then all was silent. I stayed where I was and wept over that poor, frightened cat, trapped inside. Why, I accused myself, had I cut off her exit?

Multi-layered, my sister had said. I pull out that word I had tucked away. Such an apt description of conundrums: a little girl conquered and victorious; a young student humiliated and jubilant; a gifted mentor writ large and rendered small; a teacher who controlled in one setting and advocated in another; a feral creature trapped and freed.

Am I close to Rilke's invitation? Not yet. I'm still fearful to be found ill-informed or mistaken. If I could release my death grip on failure, maybe the unknown could become an adventure. What to do? Keep walking with mystery. It weighs less than air. Bide my time. Have patience with locked doors and foreign tongues and wild creatures. Remember a wise mother and father, who let their frightened child stay home from school. Live the questions. Maybe the white light of an answer will enter me, and I won't even notice the warmth.

Rest in Bedlam

*That, at the sound of the bell, they shall go at once
to the prescribed exercises, obeying the signal as if it
were God's own voice.*

Our family album fixes her in time: a 1945 photo of my
mother, Marjorie Antoinette Warnick Kennedy. At a
bridal reception for her younger sister, she wears a cloche hat
with dark printed band and a velvet dress that drapes gracefully on her slender figure. She sits at a serving table covered
with a white cloth with an overlay of lace. The white table
centerpiece combines candles with a bouquet of gladioli and
hyacinths.

My mother, holding silver tongs, prepares to drop sugar cubes into a china cup. Sterling silver twinkles: forks,
spoons, and a tureen on a tray, the table setting is ready for
House Beautiful. She is herself in this photo, not relegated to
a role as the wife of unpredictable Dr. James Charles Kennedy or the harried mother of Mary, Michael, Antoinette,
and Alan, children born eighteen months apart from 1939-

1945. In this photo she occupies her private world of order, elegance, and safety.

In early December of 1951, a Northwest storm hit. We were living in Eugene, Oregon, and high winds pounded us, spit water through our farmhouse window crevices, and slashed branches off our cherry tree. The kitchen darkened except for candles my mother had lit. Looking out the window, we saw my father (clad in his trademark white shirt with sleeves rolled up, tie, woolen slacks, and brown dress shoes), drag a ladder from the barn, set it into the mud outside, climb the ladder wobbling in the wind, and stretch high toward the garage's empty outlet. "What is he doing, changing a light in this weather?" Mike said. As my father screwed in the bulb, a flash of electricity burst in an aura around his lean body. Then, a gust of wind toppled the ladder, jerked his hand free, and tossed him to the ground. He staggered into the kitchen, and my mother wrapped a blanket around his shoulders.

With my father, another sort of storm often brewed around the corner. He may have taught us a love for music and poetry, for chess and golf, for dinner conversation and humor, but these gifts demanded a price. His good mood one moment turned angry the next. What triggered his anger? His fury could follow a sliced shot off the tee. He could make a cruel comment about my mother's weight or fly off the handle at a referee's decision in a boxing match. Picnics ended badly when the campfire wouldn't light or the car, running on empty, wouldn't start. Rarely did Christmas pass without his accompanying melancholy or a blow-up at the dinner table. Mixed in with my love and worry for him lurked a fear of explosion.

Enveloping him in safety and keeping the family in balance was my mother's impossible challenge. In tranquility or turbulence, she read to us at night. I'd snuggle into the covers, push fear deep, and sail with the well-prepared owl and the pussycat who "went out to sea/In a beautiful pea-green boat." Unlike my parents, these two partners had planned for the trip, bringing honey and money wrapped up in a five-pound note. Fairy tales and rhymes carried me on Mother Goose wings to a safer place where the jagged pieces fell into place and my mother did not have to struggle to keep us together.

That's what I always hoped. And my mother was the eternal optimist, believing that faithfulness could expel my father's demons, hoping for the impossible.

Convent life was the opposite of what I experienced at home. The dependable seasons merged with the convent's utter predictability. From October through March, sun, rain, and snow combined to transform trees from verdant green to fiery red, before they shed tired leaves, and flickered green once again. In April and May, fruit trees burst with blossoms big as popcorn balls. From June through September, the trees produced cherries and plums and apples. Dependable evergreens shaded the station path winding behind the novitiate building and up the hill to the grotto. Ivy clung to the brick main house; hydrangea, azalea, and rhododendron lined the cloister walks; and roses set deep roots in the sunken garden. Trees and bushes, flowers and fruit lived in rhythm with us postulants, novices, and professed sisters who called The Hill our home.

Typhoon Freda or the Columbus Day Storm, hit the Pacific Northwest the evening of October 12, 1962. Around 5:00 p.m., a Friday, six of us canonical novices left the chapel and crossed the driveway to the refectory and kitchen, as we did throughout the week. A gale sideswiped us, our white veils turning us into sailboats. We pulled at our long skirts whipping around our legs, threatening to trip us. Fueled by Freda, the storm raged wildly.

Soon, wind screamed outside and rain splattered, but aided by ritual and the bell, convent life flowed serenely. We folded towels, set tables with milk pitchers and butter plates, filled teapots, ladled fish casserole and warmed-over lima beans into food tins, and loaded them onto carts. Even in the midst of a storm, one of the nuns pushed her shoulder against the door and headed outside. One hand secured her black skirts. The other hand lifted the large metal bell to call the sisters to dinner. Professed sisters, black skirts swirling, black veils blown about, hurried from chapel or along the cloister walk connecting the front and back pathways to the refectory and kitchen. Doors banged, hinges groaned. Sister John Aloysius called our names, making sure no one was left stranded in the storm.

When the lights went out, Sister gathered us around her. "Order is Heaven's first law," she said, and sent the sacristans to chapel to bring back candles, vigil lights, and candelabras. Once our improvised light source flared, we stood in the dining room and watched the devastation outside. Sheets of rain lashed across hunched evergreens, the lone swirling willow tree outside the chaplain's quarters, and the sad, twitching ivy on the brick estate.

If neighbors had braved the storm worrying about the good nuns at Palatine Hill, they would have peered through the great stretches of window and seen that our life continued as usual: month-old postulants in ankle-length black dresses, hair pulled tight behind a small black veil; first-year novices in new habits of black serge and starched white cap and white veil, the cord with its three vow knots and the large rosary hanging from the cord; second-year novices, dressed identically, but exuding a notable confidence. Neighbors would see the familiar flow of black sleeve and white napkin, genteel curve of hand and cup and nothing out of place.

Even in bedlam, rituals continued.

Sister rang the small bell that sat to the left of her water glass and said, "*Benedicamus Domino.*"

We answered, "*Deo Gratias.*"

The hum of conversation began.

Rain splashed against the glass, a prelude to more snapping, breaking outside. Pendleton's dust storms, stinging and dry, may have brought lightning to split the sky, but they paled in comparison to Freda's pandemonium. Inside, though, order prevailed. When the bell rang again, all talk—even in mid-sentence—ended. True to the Rule, the bell was to be obeyed as God's own voice.

Collected by silence, we carried dishes into the kitchen. Large pots of water steamed on the huge gas stoves. By candlelight, novices helped postulants clear tables, store food, mold butter scraps into a new cube, wash dishes, scrub pots and pans, wipe off foil and cellophane and hang them out to dry, sweep and spot the floors, and finally, even in the dark, to make sure the stainless-steel counters were streak-free. All the while the wind howled, and slates flew off the roof of the main house and gym.

Wind hurled us along the cloister walk past damaged hydrangea bushes and into the corridors of the novitiate building, down one flight of stairs, along another darkened hallway, and into the community room for recreation. Without electricity, Mozart didn't play, but candles burned on the tables and on the bookshelves. Knitting needles clicked and playing cards slapped. Jigsaw puzzlers bent their heads near-er to the candlelight. Outside, bark splintered, the flag pole chain clanged, and rain clawed at the building. The commu-nity, though, was collected and safe inside.

A novice walked to the bookshelf and picked up the small brass bell. One ring and Night Silence began. We did not line up to cross the hall into our small chapel, but said Office by candlelight in the community room. Psalms of Compline promised that the dark night, the wild beast, the violent storm, and the fiery flames would never hurt us. In the palm of God's hand we remained, at rest even in bedlam.

Saturday morning the bell awakened us. We processed up the cloister walk, through the main house, and into main chapel. Hand bells rang during Mass and throughout the rest of the day. Time seemed of little consequence—there was

only ritual, the storm, its aftermath, and a space where stillness reigned.

Outside, air sparkled with primeval newness, but trees,
branches, and debris covered the station path, the walks, and
the road. Slates from the roof had broken windows on one
side of the gym, and shattered windows in the main chapel and in the priest's house. The storm had turned secure
nature into a jumble: ivy torn from the Motherhouse brick
exterior, a split walnut tree in the orchard, a cluster of trees
cradling a lone pine, towering firs ripped out of the earth. In
their plunge, they'd crushed bushes and smashed the under-
growth. The roots of these giants hung like broken rubber
bands. The chaos had ravaged eighteen acres of fruit trees
and evergreens, berry and flower bushes, had darkened corridors, and had silenced the *Angelus* ringing from main chapel's electric bell tower.

Many of the storm's victims suffered far more than those
of us at Our Lady of Angels. The windstorm caused more
destruction in the Pacific Northwest than any other windstorm in history. More than thirty people lost their lives.
Peak gusts hit 150 miles per hour to cause property damage
estimated at over 220 million dollars.

All the severed trees and glass shards held a truth. The
Franciscan order invited us into rituals which offered spiritual comfort and physical security: a sense that all would be
well because we knew what to expect and when, and where to
place each towel, plate, and person. Then there was my own
particular truth. I had traded a family life of potential chaos for a community life of consistent order. The revelation

calmed me, like that blanket my mother once wrapped around my rain-soaked father.

Another October arrived in 1991: a cool, clear autumn evening, with a bit of a breeze—no rain in sight. My mother, propped up with pillows, accepted the chance, finally, that she was dying of congestive heart failure. Eyes clear, hair combed, wearing a pink nightgown (no hospital gown for her), she was still lovely, and still all of a piece.

My mother had weathered endless storms. How strange that my father's stroke gave her the chance to order her own life. They moved away from the house near the State Hospital into a cozy home with a patio and spacious back yard.

She studied art through correspondence classes, gained a teaching certificate, and acquired a reputation in small-town Pendleton as an artist and educator. All the while, she cared for her frail husband. He returned her tending with love, gratitude, and pride in what she had accomplished. Who would have known that these two would grow old together, in tranquility?

She smiled. Her blue eyes twinkled. "When I get to heaven, I plan to meet Charles and Jesus." She waited a beat. "In that order." Her eyes moved past me. She was leaving me for somewhere else.

Where was my mother now in the wide-awake realm between life and death? She was moving toward my father, crossing a bridge, all the while checking to see if the angel still followed. After years of faithful tending, she deserved safe passage.

Now, when the wind blows and the rains pummel the trees, these two storms come to mind. One storm was a memory bathed in fear: my father, surrounded by an aura of electricity, hanging in mid-air; my mother blanketing his body and bundling her children into bedtime stories. The other storm is a memory of adventure. Natural drama—howling wind, splintered trees, smashed windows—but devoid of terror. Outside chaos and inside order. Bells calling. Laughing nuns, unafraid, working a puzzle by candlelight. Thanks to teamwork, the colors took shape, and the completed picture appeared, one piece at a time.

Reading Margaret Drabble's brilliant memoir, *The Pattern in the Carpet*, invited me to consider why puzzles played an integral role in her childhood and a non-existent one in mine. We had chess and checkers, Monopoly and cribbage, but no puzzles. And at that convent card table, I never knew quite how to participate. Drabble's writing hums with warm scenes of a child and an auntie sharing books and solving puzzles, but the book is also a scholarly history of, and thoughtful reflection on, jigsaw puzzles. What caught me off guard was the author's reference to research into children from chaotic backgrounds, those who had trouble with puzzles because they didn't realize that fitting the frame together was the first step. A little curtain of insight fluttered open. No surprise all those years ago, that I stayed on the outside looking in.

Recently I attempted what I could not do long ago. I added an extra leaf to the dining room table to make room for a 500-piece puzzle of a village celebration. I emptied the box and flipped the pieces right-side up, my eyes seeking an orderly beginning. I needed to make a conscious effort to study the box cover: storefront signs for the "Bakery" and "Haberdashery," carnival clowns, and the terrier romping in the city park. I promised myself that I would not get seduced by bright colors and would not grab at orange and gold pieces. To become a true puzzle person, I had to patiently set aside the sedate blue and gray sky pieces and begin the essential first part of the process: snap together all the straight edges and give the puzzle an ordered frame.

Take Charge

That they cheerfully undergo labor and vexation,
and be persuaded that their work is most acceptable
to God.

My father pushed himself from early morning until late at night as a general practitioner, anesthesiologist, and pathologist. He lived in a by-gone era of handwritten case studies and Dictaphones, endless office hours, and late-night house calls. Without saying it, my father taught me that work was a matter of obligation.

In his office in downtown Eugene, young mothers arrived in the latest styles, and old men sat in ragged coats and scuffed shoes. Adjacent to the office was my father's wood-paneled, book-lined study, and once in a while, I got to sit in his huge black leather chair, touch his gigantic mahogany desk, and breathe in the smell of Raleigh cigarettes and leather book covers. On the wall hung a gold-framed painting of a boy with dark curly hair, dressed in bright red velvet. Under the moonlight, he reclined against an enormous rock, a resting spot high above the rest of the world. If I sat in the chair long enough, I could disappear into the painting, and enter a world that seemed so right for my father: another century, a royal child who had discovered a secret spot where no one could find him. And when he did hop off the rock, he would skip down the hill, and right around the bend was his castle. Maybe my father disappeared into the picture as well each time he sat at his desk, and settled, free from obligation, into a cleft beneath the moon. This room of wood and leather, study and quiet, was his home away from home.

His Eugene workday could last through the night. When the phone rang, I woke up, and if it was my turn to keep him company, dressed quickly, and leashed the dog. I took the blanket my mother held out. She turned to my father with a sigh. "Charles, why is it you are forever on call?"

We drove into the countryside until we came to a small house whose porch light revealed peeling green paint and a beat-up chair. "Stay in the car, kiddo," my father said. "Get some sleep." He lifted his black medical bag, locked the car, and headed toward the house. I was not afraid, nestled under the blanket, stars overhead, and Cookie cuddled close, but I hoped he wouldn't be too long. I wanted to stay awake until my father returned, but my eyes drooped. It seemed only minutes later that he opened the car door and said, "We're off, kiddo." I'd fallen asleep thinking about my father, who answered the phone and drove out late to help people.

Labor as a burden was a lesson Catholic school continued to teach. Textbook illustrations showed a sad Adam and Eve driven from paradise, their heads bent in shame and their skin covered by animal hides. Since Adam and Eve disobeyed, they would have to work—not any kind, but work that made them sweat. Like the first parents and a tired father, I, too, had to work.

Not right away, though.

A memory of regular chores begins no earlier than my eleventh year in the one-level house in Pendleton, Oregon. My mother and Mary washed laundry and hung it out to dry. They ironed napkins and handkerchiefs, shirts and shorts, dresses and slacks. Mike mowed the grass, raked leaves, and cleaned up the "dog dirt" from our spaniels and the neighbors' mutts. Alan and I escaped essential jobs. I did stack dishes, run the vacuum, and make my bed, and even these small chores proved a bother.

I brought this questionable work ethic to the convent. Within the first week, the six of us postulants were deployed to the cramped, unbearably hot third floor of the main house. Fifty summer school sisters had left The Hill in August to return to teaching jobs. Our task was to take apart the beds. Sister Emerita, elderly and wiry, demonstrated how to dismantle the metal bed frames. Perhaps she heard me groan with one more swing of the hammer or complain during the hammering, hauling, and stacking the frames as well as separating and packaging screws, nuts, and bolts. What I do recall are her words: "Sisters, you are not tired until you are finished."

As postulants and novices, we had a charge assigned to us for the entire year. I got latrine duty. Pretty funny, I thought, that I had the same job as Andy Griffith's character in *No Time for Sergeants*. Maybe I could rig toilet lids to pop up in salute. Instead, mornings from 7:50 until 8:20, I casually swished a rag around six sinks, two bathtubs, two showers, and four toilets. I pushed a broom over the floor and polished the metal door plate (checking my reflection on the only surface resembling a mirror). Most days I quit early.

One morning, as I opened the bathroom door to leave, Sister John Aloysius appeared, saying, "Antoinette, let's see how you clean." She walked to the open window, took out her handkerchief, drew it across the ledge, and turned toward me. Dust formed like a gray caterpillar on the white cloth. Next, she turned on the water in the sink. "Do you see that, Antoinette?"

"What, Sister?"

"The film that covers this sink." She rolled up her sleeves, sprinkled Bon Ami, and scrubbed until the porcelain sparkled and water flowed smoothly over the surface. Sister checked the shower stalls and the bathtubs. Once again, film appeared when she ran the water. Even I saw the bathtub rings. After scrubbing them clean, she frowned. "What would your mother say?"

Sister moved into the toilet stalls. "This is a disgrace." She stepped out, got the Bon Ami, filled the bucket with water, and stepped back inside. "Hold the stall door open." Sister hoisted up her habit, rolled up her wide sleeve, knelt, put her hand inside the toilet bowl, and began to scrub— without rubber gloves. "This is how you clean." When she finished, she eyed me with a relentless gaze. "Cleanliness is next to Godliness. When sickness spreads, it can be traced to the kitchen and bathroom."

I knelt on the bathroom floor, folded my hands, and said, "I humbly beg a penance for not keeping the bathroom clean."

Her mouth formed a straight line. "Take responsibility, woman."

Sister turned away. When the bathroom door swung shut, I stood up and looked around. The clean sink and the image of Sister scrubbing the toilet with her bare hands shook loose a resolution: I could do this.

The bathroom became mine—a porcelain palace. Responsibility, the "ability to respond," took on a meaning which I embraced. When Sister John Aloysius appeared unannounced over the next month, sinks and bathtubs sparkled. When she stood on tiptoe to run her handkerchief over the top of the door, no creepy-crawly fuzz ever soiled the white cloth. At her last visit, she smiled and said, "Well done, Antoinette."

As much as I gained from the art of "convent clean," I had not expected too much work during our canonical year (our second year as novices) because we were to dedicate ourselves to prayer and studying the black book of directives—the Rule and Constitutions. Well, we did attend theology classes. We did listen to Sister's directions on the Rule. But the rest of the year we worked. We took our turn to hang over a huge sink and scour pots, pans, and kettles. We scrubbed, on our hands and knees, terrazzo floors in kitchen and chapel, polished pews which still held last week's Johnson's Pride, and buffed the novitiate corridor with a polisher weighing more than we did. Manual labor from dawn to dusk.

Monday was laundry day. In the basement of the main house, we six canonicals managed the washing load for more than seventy nuns and one priest, as well as the starched cloths and coverings needed for Mass. On our feet from 6:00 in the morning until 4:00 in the afternoon, we worked as a team.

One nun ran the giant press, others the starch-and-hand-iron tasks, another the folding and organization. I filled the behemoth washer, loaded wet clothes into the extractor, hauled the spun laundry into the dryer, and in between times, guided spreads and sheets through a monstrous ironer called the mangle. We carried wicker baskets and galvanized tubs of clean laundry up flights of stairs to bedrooms, dormitories, and sacristy. Our reward was early bedtime.

Canonical year was also the year of special assignments: linen room, sewing room, and the sacristy. Sister chose the most careful and efficient novices. Since I had received none of the favored charges, part of me was miffed, but the other part grateful that I didn't have the responsibility. Then, after the Columbus Day storm, Sister John Aloysius called me over. "I'm putting you in the sacristy, Sister." There were no further details, all I knew was that one of my set was out of this important position, and I was in. I did not ask Sister John Aloysius for an explanation. I did not encourage her to reconsider. Instead, I thanked her as though the assignment were a privilege.

On the first day, the second-year novice and head sacristan gave me a tour. One closet contained cleaning supplies, vases, and garden clippers. In others, Mass vestments hung: purple for Lent, white for Easter, gold for Christmas, red for martyrs, and green for the other days. Drawers held neck stoles and tabernacle covers that matched the vestments. Under the sink sat glass cruets for the water and wine, and in the cabinets above, the sacred chalices and ciboria cups for the hosts. "Sister," the head sacristan advised, "no altar boys are at Mass. If anything goes wrong, the responsibility is all yours." Sister pointed out candelabras, tapers, the incense holder, and polish. She opened the missal to demonstrate how to mark the reading for the priest. On our way out, she directed me into the sanctuary where the red lamp burned. She touched the base of the candle. "Sister, we let the candle burn low, but we never, ever, let the sanctuary lamp burn out." My stomach knotted. Too much to remember. Too much to forget.

Catholic Mass was theater and my two years as a sacristan a study in stage fright. If a mistake occurred, like a cruet without water, I rose with disciplined posture and silent shoes, and solved the problem. Thankfully, we made few mistakes, mainly because of my companion novices. The first year, I was assistant to a highly organized nun. The second year, when I was in charge, I had a helper who possessed humor and resilience. We arranged bouquets and mopped a flooded basement, climbed into rafters to change a light, and when the electricity blew, operated the chimes manually. Two years free of big mistakes—almost.

Following Easter week in 1964, and three months before I ended the sacristan stint, we two nuns had put in a full day's work organizing closets and drawers, cleaning candelabras, and wiping the sanctuary's marble pillars and steps. At the back of chapel, I turned to admire our finished work. One darkened corner met my eye. I blinked. I looked again, but there was no doubt that I, second-year novice and head sacristan, had done the unthinkable: I had let the sanctuary lamp burn out.

I stared at the space, willing the candle to flicker. Nothing. Only a bright stab of pain between my eyes. "What should we do?" I fretted.

"Go replace the candle," my sacristy partner said.

Of course.

Convent rigor, whether it took place in the latrine, laundry, or sacristy taught me the basics of responsibility. In religious boot camp, I toughened muscles, both physical and emotional and discovered energy I did not know I possessed. Mistakes happened, but no skies split open. Only a distant echo of my father's voice, *For the love of Mike, stop worrying. Replace the candle.*

More essential to the question of labor, I found that I *wanted* to give the sisters a spotless bathroom, laundry washed and folded with care, not to mention Mass celebrated without distraction. I found happiness in rolling up my sleeves and taking charge.

Over fifty years ago, in a classroom filled with afternoon sun and fifty-three third graders, I asked the children to describe a favorite object in the classroom. Molly loved the statue of Mary in the corner by the front window, and Jeff liked the soccer ball tucked away in the closet. Jennifer treasured the agate collection on the back ledge. Stephen said, "My favorite object is the door. In the afternoon at three o'clock, I get to walk out of it." At the dismissal bell, this little boy (who had endured another day of coloring phonics sheets and staying within the lines) lined up with the others, took his jacket from the cloakroom, and was gone, running across the playground. Maybe when he arrived home, he threw off his uniform, and got into jeans and T-shirt. With a comic book and Twinkie in hand, he climbed high into his treehouse—a 1965 version of the young boy in red velvet.

Not long ago, I mentioned the painting to Mary and Michael and discovered that my mother had not only designed my father's study, but had specifically chosen Sir Thomas Lawrence's *The Red Boy* and hung the artwork where my father could enjoy it. I imagined him at his desk, writing out medical notes or recording a diagnosis on the Dictaphone. He would have looked up once in a while to see the lad high on a mountain, removed from a demanding world. First, though, the metaphorical bed frames had to be stacked neatly, and the bolts and screws collected, and they almost never were.

No question my temperament has led me, in many ways, down the path walked by my father. I have worked compulsively and longed for respite. Yet, unlike him, I have not had a family for whom to provide, nor financial ruin, nor addictions to sap creativity and energy. Thanks to the Franciscans, talent, and good luck, I have had the hours and the economic security to weave a teaching career of which, for the most part, I am proud. My most fulfilling job, though, occurred in retirement, and had nothing to do with education.

Three days a week, beginning at eight in the morning and ending at noon, I volunteered at a local animal shelter. Opening the door guaranteed me barking, howling greetings, as well as the pungent smell of urine, feces, and untouched day-old dog food moistened with slops from dirty water bowls. One by one, the dog walkers appeared with the looped, braided leashes. Letting themselves slip sideways into the cages, they crooned to the pups, leading their shy or ecstatic charges out from confinement and out of the building. As each cage emptied, my work began. I wiped up the feces and urine, put the soiled bedding in the laundry, scrubbed the floors, and hosed down the cage, using a dry mop before putting fresh laundry and supplies into each enclosure. One room at a time the smell of detergent and Lysol eclipsed stale odors. One dog at a time re-entered a sparkling space newly supplied with fresh water, kibble, and fluffy blankets.

Once, at the end of the volunteer stint, I felt the supervisor's eyes on me as I wrung the mops, scrubbed out the bucket, and disposed of the rags. She approached me and said, "You're the best worker we've ever had. And so thorough. Where did you ever learn to clean like that?"

Crown with Fire

*That they remember the best and safest discipline
consists in obedience, in regular observance, in self-
denial, and in that charity which is patient, is kind,
beareth all things, endureth all things.*

In late 1951, the four of us Kennedy kids sat in the movie
theater in downtown Eugene and waited for the lights to
dim and the red velvet curtain to rise on the Technicolor epic
Quo Vadis. Robert Taylor flaunted his Roman military regalia
and Deborah Kerr her pink robes. Peter Ustinov ranted and
fiddled and the Christians sang as lions tore them apart. That
day I saw in living color that the body could be eaten alive,
yet the soul would go to heaven. God loves terrible sacrifice.

That's what six weeks of Lent celebrated. On Ash
Wednesday I knelt at the altar railing, felt the priest's thumb
mark a sooty cross on my forehead. *Memento homo, quia pulvis
es, et in pulverem revertis,"* he said. Yes, I *was* dust and would go
back to dust, so we had to make restitution. We Kennedy
kids sacrificed Heath Bars and Milk Duds, Black Crows and

Baby Ruths, and stashed the candy in four piles arranged in the hallway drawer. At last, Holy Week arrived, and the countdown began to Holy Saturday, the official end of Lent. Mary doled the candy into our hands, and each of us found a secret place to enjoy the rewards of our sacrifice.

At Our Lady of Angels convent, I learned a new word for sacrifice. Mortification was "the subjection and denial of bodily passions and appetites by abstinence or self-inflicted pain or discomfort." Its meaning was reinforced every day, again with something sweet. On each table in the dining room sat a stainless-steel sugar bowl. We did not pass the bowl to one another, and we did not spoon out any for ourselves. The sugar bowl stayed where it was, meal after meal, untouched. On Saturdays, we broke up the lumps and set the container back in place. Sister John Aloysius used the sugar as a symbol for sacrifice. "Learn to wait," she said. "Delay gratification." When I looked at the sugar bowl and wasn't even tempted to sprinkle a teaspoon on my cereal, I knew I'd come a long way since the Heath Bar and Milk Duds days.

Most of the novitiate's daily acts of denial centered on food. While the professed sisters ate fresh meat and vegetables, we postulants and novices consumed left-over turnips, spinach, cauliflower, and lima beans. To stem any complaints, Sister John Aloysius turned our attention to the Rule: "If the food given them is not to their taste, they should not murmur, but by patiently bearing what is disagreeable, they shall merit a heavenly reward." Writing home, I did not divulge how much I missed my mother's goulash and chicken pot pies. Never complain. Control the body and mortify it.

In convent celebrations, however, food took front and center, and denial sat in a far corner. Our Constitutions read, "On certain feasts during the year, the Sisters shall be allowed a special treat at table, as the Superior thinks fit, to promote a salutary joy in God." No matter if the celebration was for Christmas, Easter, or July Fourth, the atmosphere turned jubilant and the menu delicious. For breakfast we had steaming coffee (not tea), grapefruit dotted with maraschino cherries, cinnamon rolls, scrambled eggs, ham, and bacon. For dinner we feasted on pork chops and applesauce, or hamburgers and French fries. Platters held pear and peach slices, ice cream, strawberry-rhubarb pie, and cookies, cookies, cookies. The ritual evoked memories of my childhood Holy Saturday: the truer the sacrifice, the sweeter the reward.

Despite those celebratory feasts, mortification was ever-present. Denial of the flesh dealt with more than what was on our dinner plates. Under the heading "Fasting, Abstinence, and works of Corporal Austerities," the final requirement stated, "All Wednesdays and Fridays, the Sisters shall take the discipline, unless, because of a feast, or for some other reason, it is anticipated or deferred." The "discipline" was the ritual performed by the novices (not the postulants) and like all the professed sisters throughout our Franciscan order, I followed the directive.

In my cell I made sure to pull the curtain tight. From the bottom drawer, I pulled out the wrapped "discipline,"

a foot-long, waxed, braided whip. I whispered the prayer
"Salve Regina", the gentle hymn to Mary, Mother of Mercy.
I hit my body. Of course, the soft waxen cords did not break
the skin and no blood flowed. I prayed to Mary to grant me,
sinful daughter of Eve, the courage to pass through this valley of tears. When I finished the prayer, I wrapped up the
discipline and tucked it away in the drawer.

Another mortification, Particular Examen, occurred
each day at noon. I knelt with all the postulants and novices in the novitiate chapel, and pulled out a small notebook.
With the eraser-less pencil, I plotted my predominant faults
and their resolutions: do not offer an opinion of how things
should be; refuse to admire yourself on reflective surfaces;
don't look around in curiosity; eat more Brussels sprouts
than usual; compliment the sister I envy; take the smaller
piece of dessert. The purpose of this exercise was to choose
any one of these as a focus for the week.

In childhood, I had a recurring dream of a big, ugly man
chasing me through alleyways. My legs moved in slow-motion. Before his hairy arm grabbed me, I awoke. Early one
morning, I sat upright, terrified. *Next time,* I promised, *I'll turn
around and look that bully in the eye.* Next time happened—same
alleys, same leaden legs. I ran into a Safeway (even without
an interpreter, I got the connection), and the boogeyman
followed. Standing in the check-out line, I turned around
and faced him. That horrible creature smiled, waved, and
said, "Hi." The dream never recurred. Particular Examen
was like my dream: turn around, face your failings, and partner honesty with discipline.

One afternoon, Sister Joan entered the gym with a tiny woman dressed in leotards. Even before Sister introduced her to us postulants and novices as Cornelia Cerf, a dance instructor, I recognized her as the exotic figure who once performed "Envy" in green scarves. Sister Joan continued, "Miss Cerf will teach you modern dance." Out of my disciplined regimen of the Examen prayer, deferred goals, and mortification burst a wild cheer: *I get to dance.*

I may have waltzed with my father in pajamas, but I honed dancing skills with Dick Clark's *American Bandstand* and those Philadelphia teens who dressed to the nines in skirts and sweaters, jackets and ties. On Friday nights in the church hall or after ball games in school auditoriums, I moved to the beat of Chuck Berry's "Blueberry Hill," the McGuire Sisters' "Sugartime," and Eddie Cochrain's "Summertime Blues." Nothing equaled the freedom of swaying hips and fast feet.

After the first class with Miss Cerf, I realized what I should have guessed: the classes she taught had no connection to *American Bandstand*. Her heroine was Martha Graham, the grand dame of modern dance; the guru of the body under control. Under Miss Cerf's instruction and Graham's "contraction and release," we breathed, leaned, and extended into space. We were stones, still and grounded; saplings unfolding in time-lapse. We skipped, ran, and leaped, but never rocked as with Elvis. For Miss Cerf, liberation was the partner of restraint. She said often, "Through discipline comes freedom." Under her guidance we acquired the tools of control and muscle, balance and bone. And she said that our white veils and long black habits with wide sleeves were the perfect garb for performance.

To fulfil the requirements of the class, we needed to perform, and to that purpose Miss Cerf selected the prayer of Shadrach, Meshach, and Abednego in the book of Daniel. Each of us chose a scripture line and movement from the litany of praise for sun and moon, stars and rain, lightning and clouds. Miss Cerf demanded that we visually proclaim our dance beyond the narrow boundaries of a stage. No meek outreach of hand or arm or torso, but an extension, an elasticity that forced the gesture to stretch. And, no abrupt end. Allow the movement to continue its transition of elegance and strength.

The auditorium filled that day with sisters who lived at The Hill, but also Lewis & Clark students. Were the other novices self-conscious or anxious about performing for an audience of our peers? Our own nuns would be an easy group to please, but college students majoring in music and art and dance?

Once the crowd hushed and the scripture words were proclaimed, our dance acquired a life of its own. With hands lifted, we called upon angels and nature to give praise and thanks to God.

Sleeves swayed into wings and wind. White veils formed sea foam and snowflakes. Black skirts mimicked the rush of darkness and clash of thunder. Bless the Lord: praise and exalt God above all forever. The psalm ended. We clasped hands; we bowed. With the applause, we united with a world we had relinquished, attired in stage costumes blessed by the bishop, and spinning free through strict control.

Three years I spent in the studio of the disciplined life. Mortification, self-examination, sacrifice, and dance shaped my spirit and body. Contract, release, breathe, and bend. Spring into the unexpected. Come back to earth. I memorized the roles of athlete and martyr, performer and ascetic, and thrived in the consistent and ordered regimen.

Stir the sugar grains inside the silver bowl. Leave the sweetness for another day.

When did community rules change so that I no longer whipped this sinful body of mine? Not too long after I left the novitiate, but the stories continued, even after twenty-five years. At a lunch gathering in the late 1980s, a group of us former nuns laughed about the secret practice of the discipline.

One said, "The novitiate was enough of a penance. I barely tapped myself."

Another added, "Beat myself? Are you kidding? I hit the chair."

Not me. I hit myself and hit myself hard.

A few years ago, I watched a documentary on the ultra-runners in Death Valley who participate in a July race covering 135 miles of asphalt in temperatures rising to 120 degrees. I thought, *What kind of nutcase would do this?*

When interviewed, the runners said that Death Valley is the ultimate challenge to see what the mind and body can accomplish. I wouldn't think of going there, even in a Subaru packed with water bottles or even to reap stories to last a lifetime.

In ways, though, I seek kinship with the lean, lithe athletes who endure a journey up an 8,000-foot elevation, up a barren slope, like Jesus in the desert, like Jesus carrying his cross up Golgotha. Back I go again to the familiar ground of self-denial, taming the body, freeing the spirit—the mountain of family, the Church, convent, and cell. In "Little Gidding," T.S. Eliot writes of another journey requiring that the traveler be in a condition of a simplicity that costs everything. Then all things will be well, when "the tongues of flame are in-folded/Into the crowned knot of fire." Miss Cerf and Eliot share a similar wisdom: discipline is a flame that sears us, strips us, and then sets us free.

The discipline I follow now is the practice of yoga. I am faithful not out of mortification, but more out of fear. My spine could curve, like the lady who shuffles in downtown Portland, struggling to navigate burrito wrappers and soda cans. Fragile bones and osteoporosis remind me that the crowned knot of fire takes different forms. Daily I slip the *Essential Adagios* CD into my player and lie down on flannel blankets. Strains of Barber and Beethoven accompany the pull of muscle and bone. When Dvorak's "New World Symphony" begins, my back muscles slowly relax, and the melody hums in my brain. *Going Home, going home.* My breathing slows. *Work all done, care laid by.* For a short while, my bones align and my spine heals. Through discipline comes freedom.

One day my soul will burst free—as Christians believe. I'm promised a vast dance floor where I'll sway like a willow and leap like a gazelle. And afterwards? Old Testament Proverbs adds that Wisdom has set a table with fine wine and delicious meat, so I'll mosey on in and take a seat. If I'm wrong and neither dancing nor a feast are my rewards, maybe a more exquisite surprise waits. No reason to limit the infinite. For now, discipline awakens me out of the familiar. She propels me through barren lands, lets me rest in meadows, and nudges me along mountain passes I never would have chosen on my own.

Return

And the end of all our exploring
Will be to arrive from where we started
And know the place for the first time.
                    T.S. Eliot, "Little Gidding"

Forget Your Father's House

That they shall not go into the houses of seculars un-
less they are ordered to do so or unless they have
special permission to do so.

In moments of unhappiness, my mother said, "I refuse to poison my life with regrets." My father let himself yearn for "what might have been." Since the convent took my mother's side, I was caught between the two approaches: whenever melancholy told me that I did not belong in community, my optimism held on to the convent's awesome rituals. What nagged from the first to the last year, though, was homesickness, shoved into a corner like a Raggedy Ann doll. At moments I longed, when no one was looking, to straighten her pinafore, and tie a new bow in her yarn hair.

At first, when the Franciscan order cautioned us to keep an emotional distance from our blood families, the caveat had little effect. Palatine Hill Road wound down to Terwilliger Boulevard and to my Aunt Ginny and Uncle George.

On the convent property stood the green water tower that Uncle Bob had helped engineer. Students from Lewis & Clark College studied on the convent lawn, and I planned to ask them if they knew the Portland Kennedys, my cousins who'd attended Central Catholic, Jesuit, and St. Mary's. Plus, in the first week I had visits from relatives.

When homesickness did arise, the ache twisted its way through my stomach and into my heart. Letters repeated the phrases, "Please write," "I miss you so much." Sister John Aloysius reiterated her belief: *the best way to deal with homesickness is not to dwell on it. Talking about it is infectious.* I tried to follow her advice. Life wasn't that great back in Pendleton, I told myself, so don't make the past ideal when it wasn't. In an attempt to release a longing for home, I turned to the Gospel passage from Luke:

> *"To another, Jesus said, 'Follow me,' but he replied, 'Let me go first and bury my father.' But Jesus answered, 'Let the dead bury the dead.' And another said, 'I will follow you, Lord, but first let me say farewell to my family at home.' Jesus said, 'No one who sets his hand to the plow and looks to what was left behind is fit for the kingdom of God.'"*

At eighteen, I believed I had to surrender blood ties. Praying the psalms only reinforced the importance of separation. "Hearken, O daughter, and see, and incline thy ear: and forget thy people and thy father's house." The biblical words were not a metaphor. If I looked back and if I pined for home, I was not worthy to follow Jesus Christ. But memories of my past life sneaked into the present moment.

In place of my leisurely bubble bath of Jean Nate spice and flower scent, I had a white enamel bucket, ivory soap, and not a minute to spare. I filled the bucket with water and waited in silence for an empty bathroom stall. Quickly. Do not keep another waiting, I scrubbed under my arms, between my toes, crotch, and buttocks. Soap scum rose to the top of the water.

Squirming into my nightgown, I emptied the bucket and flushed the toilet, grabbed my belongings, left the stall, and practicing "custody of the eyes," stood in line for an empty sink. When my turn came, I brushed my teeth, aware of using only a little toothpaste and water. I finished, rinsed out the sink, hurrying, hurrying back to my cell before the signal for lights out.

By joining community, I sacrificed individuality. One day in study hall, I flipped through the 1955 centenary book of the Franciscan Sisters. Group photos featured nuns gathered outside schools and hospitals, inside recreation rooms, and at Mass. The pictures reminded me of the famous penguin photos. Four of them, all in black and white, face the same direction, feet poised identically, and ready to venture across the street. Could penguins be taught to don aprons and hold a paring knife? Maybe they could peel potatoes for a hundred plus nuns. With patience, we could teach them to haul containers and sweep floors. Then they could strut out of the building, like a phalanx of nuns, all together.

My mother would not have understood constant togetherness. "Take time alone," she used to say. "Learn to be your own best company." I missed hiking solo on the sunburned hill outside our house, missed hitting golf balls and retrieving them. I missed coming into the kitchen all by myself to smear apple slices with peanut butter. I missed being in bright sun or starred darkness with no one but my own best company. Those days had ended. As one organism, we sisters prayed, sang, ate, worked, studied, and recreated because our energy and focus belonged to the community. I learned to navigate each day in the first-person plural.

I anticipated and dreaded visiting days. If my family had been like the others and capable of walking the grounds; if they hadn't looked tired and worn and old; if they were sociable and not private, maybe I wouldn't have minded. Visiting days followed a familiar pattern. I stood in the huge middle refectory that connected the novitiate dining room with that of the professed. My mother parked the pink Mercury directly in front so that my father had a short distance to drag his limp right leg. Alan helped him as he struggled with the walker.

Never did this scene play out without nuns around. The sisters commented, "What a trial for your mother." Or, "Your dear brother. Such a good son to stay with your parents." Then, "God bless your poor father." Angry at having my family on public display, I forgot that these nuns, many from Ireland, had relinquished their families, and had suffered—more than I—the plight of the homesick.

In keeping with convent regulations, the nuns served my family a lunch I was not allowed to share. After the visiting period ended, my mother, father, and brother got back in the car, ready to make the 220-mile trip back to Pendleton. I wanted to slip into a corner and sink into sadness. Instead, I cleared the lunch dishes, thanked the sisters for their help, and quietly counted the months until the next visit.

A name to live by helped define our family, and that name was Kennedy. As a child, I imbibed my parents' pride in our surname and my father's desire to return home to Galway. One day, he promised, we would claim the Kennedy castle. I pictured the expanse of stone and turret waiting for us, just over the hill. As I grew older and no trip to Ireland materialized, I began to doubt such visions of nobility and wondered if my mother actually believed we had a castle to claim. What was not in question was her love for being Mrs. Charles Kennedy. "Be proud of your family name, children," she said. "You have only one."

Soon enough, the Kennedy surname would be of little importance. As part of the investing ritual, each woman received the white veil and a new title, the "name of a saint with the word 'Sister' prefixed." We would not be Sister Mary Rose Smith, but Sister Mary Rose. Last names ended up in files for official documents, but last names no longer were included in everyday life or a cause for bloodline reference.

In the excitement of getting a new name, I forgot my father's pride in being a Kennedy. (I had, a while ago, discounted the Galway castle). Instead, I gloried in the coming change. "Since the next time I write, my name will be different, I sign this letter with all my love, Antoinette, Toni, Theresa, Kennedy." Goodbye to the inherited name. Hello to the chosen one.

Sister John Aloysius warned us there was no guarantee we would receive any of our choices and to beware of wanting a particular name inordinately. As a sign of my holy indifference, I chose less favorite names, but wanted to acknowledge my family: Sister Maria Charles, Sister Michael Ignatius, and Sister Daniel Mary. It did trouble me that whatever name I got, I'd be stuck with it until death.

On investing day, August of 1962, we postulants, dressed in simple, white dresses and white net veils, processed into the main chapel for a Mass ceremony packed with families, friends, and nuns from the entire Province. The choir sang *Veni Sponsa Christi* (Come, Bride of Christ) while the bishop handed each of us the folded habit.

In the back of the sanctuary, we dressed in serge, white cap, white veil, waist cord with three knots, and brown Franciscan rosary. Out the back sanctuary exit we walked, then processed in again, garbed in the "habit of religion." When Mass ended, we received our new titles. My disappointment startled me.

On that humid summer day, I joined my family under a plum tree. All at once, the habit had turned cumbersome. I yearned for cutoffs and my hair to hang free. To go home. My mother beamed—proud of her daughter, the nun. "Toni, you look beautiful." I tried to smile, but the starched cap would not give.

"My name is Sister Miriam Michael now."

My father's face crumpled. Was it from sadness or from pride in his daughter, or the effects of the stroke? My mother caught herself. "That's lovely, dear."

Under the leafy fruit tree, the gap widened between us. On one side the Kennedys. On the other, the new nun. I had chosen a different name and a different family. No turning back.

That evening, the six of us, with white towels around our shoulders, participated in the age-old convent ritual that has its roots in the thirteenth-century legend of St. Clare, the young woman who had relinquished her family to live like St. Francis. One of the brothers cut her long, beautiful hair as a sign of her surrender to Christ.

Our turn for the shearing approached. I kept my eyes downcast. With a snip of the scissors, Connie's auburn curls fell to the floor. I felt the novice's hands as she cut my dark blond hair. As part of the ritual, we could take a more drastic step, if we wished. The novice whispered the question, and I said "Yes." The electric shaver buzzed over my scalp. Two days after investiture, I did see my reflection (a distorted one) in the chrome shower fixture, and though surprised at my small, stark head, I was not offended. The daughter in me, though, was glad that my mother could not see me. She would have cried. *Oh, Toni, sweetheart, what happened to your beautiful hair?*

✎

On a mild December day in Riverside, California, I sat in our community room with its view of the enclosed garden, pushed aside the pile of fifty phonics papers, and wrote this letter home.

"It is Christmas again, yet there is no fire burning in a huge fireplace with all six of us listening to Dickens' *Christmas Carol*. I can see every one of your faces and I can hear Scrooge and Marley, Tiny Tim, and Bob Cratchett as clearly as if it were really all happening. Why is this? Why has God given us the power, magnificent but painful, whereby we can treasure moments of the past, delight in their purity and innocence? For all you have sacrificed for me, for all the love with which you have showered me, I say Thank You from my heart. I have a wonderful family of sisters, but you are my First Family, all ways, always."

To read the letter fifty years later saddens me. At first glance the words seem to arise from a yearning not only to return home, but to send across the miles an appreciation for my family's sacrifice. From the letter emanates memories which belong to the innocence of childhood. In that light, I imagine myself as the young nun caught between her commitment to a religious community and her blood bond with family.

Yet, in between the lines lurks a shallow, shadow dimension as well. How easy to play the poet when I lived with a new family, given my own bedroom and bathroom; provided with food by our Latino cook; deemed special by the parish priest. How easy to write pious words to my mother and father when I was no longer around to share their burdens;

to express a longing for a past to which I had no intention of returning. As my parents read this letter, they may have smiled at the memories I evoked, but I am sure that my father must have said, "I told her she can always come home." His eyes would have filled, maybe he would have taken a long draw on his cigarette. "Then, why doesn't she?" And he would have reached for his walker upon which he depended, seen snow drift over Pendleton's barren hills, and touched the letter, like all the ones before it—stripped of the Kennedy name, and know why I didn't come home.

For twenty years my sister Mary researched and collected documents, stories, and photos that resulted in a magnificent book of family history—work begun by my brother Alan, and now continued by Mary's daughter, Lisa. Old photos transport us to our father's Irish connections in the Glens of Antrim and Galway and to our mother's lineage going back to the *Mayflower*, and her blood links to pioneers enduring the trek west by wagon train. Essential to the genealogy albums are the descendent charts of names—fathers and mothers, sons and daughters. Names on birth and marriage certificates are where stories begin. Names in obituaries and on tombstones are where stories end, only to start anew by those who trace the engravings.

Names are the breath of my family's precious documents, like the 1953 listing from the Blue Book Social Register of Oregon. An introductory notation defines the purpose of the register as the "official and accepted index of Oregon's leading and prominent men and women."

KENNEDY, Dr. and Mrs. James Charles
(nee Marjorie Antoinette Warnick)
U of O, U of O Med. School, Phi Beta Kappa,
Beta Theta Pi, Nu Sigma Nu, Alpha
Omega Alpha
Wife's Affiliations: Willmt. Arts& Crafts
Soc., Eug. Art Center, Port. Art Assoc,
Scl. of Art.
Jrs: Mary Paige, Antoinette Theresa, Michael
Warnick, Alan Edgar.

The listing lauds my father, and each name below his reminds me that we Kennedys may have hitched a ride on the coattails of his achievements, but each of us had, and will continue to have, our own tales that travel far beyond my father.

Given our family struggles, it would have been easy to discard the *Blue Book*, but my mother made sure the document stayed with us. Of course, she was proud to be listed in the index, and she desired, like my father, to leave her mark upon the world. But, in keeping with the spirit of ancestors, she believed there exists a unique, inimitable quality about a name in print. Perhaps that dimension of the artistic life appealed: her greeting cards, pen-and-inks, playing cards, nature scenes, and portraits all bear the signature, *M. Antoinette Kennedy*. True to what she treasured, she kept the *Social Register* on a shelf in her Pendleton home and marked it to our page. "Never forget to be proud of your family name," she reminded us. "You have only one."

Names can be forever, written in a genealogy, or maybe they stay for a while and then disappear. Maybe a title defined us in one life and disguised us in another. As part of our Franciscan congregation's renewal, we had the opportunity in 1970 to return to our birth or baptismal names. On the desk in my room rested the formal, written invitation from the general minister, and in my hand, a fountain pen. Without hesitation, I wrote my religious name: *Sister Miriam Michael*. Directly below was the line meant for the name I wished to be called. More than just a title change, my signature seemed to hold the possibility of forgiveness, a way to say how sorry I was for wandering far away from home. Would the return be that simple, or would it seem an alien replacement? Carefully I wrote, *Sister Antoinette Kennedy* and watched the ink dry. Within a heartbeat, my name smiled up at me, utterly familiar and very much at home. I heard my father say, "She's our Toni again," and the whole Kennedy clan, living and dead, circled close.

Guard the Word

That they remember that letters to parents and relatives should not be written too frequently; their sole purpose is to fulfill a filial duty.

My mother taught me exactly how a letter ought to be written. I first learned the skill when Wendy, the fairy, lived with us. She had a glass message bowl, set in the middle of the dining room table, and here we dropped a jelly bean or Life Saver. Inevitably, a thank-you note appeared, its letters inked so small we needed a magnifying glass. Wendy left us gifts: a dime for a tooth, an agate for a kindness. "No gift should go unacknowledged," my mother remarked. We wrote thank-you notes in return, our tiny words on tiny slips of paper.

As I grew older, my mother continued to guide all aspects of letter writing. I wrote thank-you notes to grandparents and aunts for Christmas and birthday gifts, for slumber parties and dinner invitations. I wrote to Mike in the Army and to Mary in college, who, even miles away, never forgot my birthday. Letter writing took place at a table, sitting in a straight-back chair, upright posture, fountain pen with blue ink, stationery (slanted just right), and wrist in Palmer position. Always write, my mother insisted, in "good light."

Once a month, on Sunday (except during Advent and Lent), we postulants and novices wrote one letter home. Our written communication had clear parameters, for it was "entirely forbidden to write letters as well as to receive them, without the permission of the Superior." This communal activity, performed during the afternoon, followed a familiar ritual: wooden table and straight-back chair, pen and stationery, hand in Palmer position, and from the wide windows, ample light. We focused on the one communication allowed us each month and addressed it to places as close as Washington State and as far away as County Cork.

Thursdays (except during Advent and Lent) in the community room, in early afternoon, I waited as Sister John Aloysius handed out the mail. Since my mother forwarded the letter (with instructions to siblings and friends to send it back to her), my one letter often reaped a harvest. Upbeat newsreels of army mail call, with the guys whooping with joy, and going off by themselves to read their letters, bore similarities to the novitiate. Except the whooping was silent. Our letters in front of us, we waited until each sister had her mail. Carefully (not too eagerly), and slowly (to make the words last), we began to read.

I imagined my mother in her small office. Like a modern-day Jane Austen, she wrote lengthy, newsy correspondence, listings of friends and sprinklings from Pendleton news and from my siblings, descriptions of silk and dotted Swiss dresses, weather, sickness, food, her art studio, and always heartfelt wishes. In that spirit, I responded. I described the convent schedule in detail. I named names, and relayed snippets about the "magnificent" weather. I asked about Mary's boyfriend, Ray, and her trip to the beach; about Alan's love life: "Hey, hon, tell about that cute frosh. By any chance is that Arlene?" I begged for more, "Please keep the letters coming!" Thanks to my mother, they did.

Our communication was inspected by Sister John Aloysius. At first, I did not consider this fact invasive, so eager was I for the connection, and crammed the one letter full of messages, not only for family, but also others. In the section for Alan, I wrote that I had heard from my former boyfriend. "Would you please tell him what my schedule is? I put it in my last letter. He wanted to know all about convent life." When I finished writing, I placed my missive in the novitiate slot, sure that my family would have it by next week.

A month later, Sister John Aloysius summoned me to her office, a small, ordered space, filled with light from two large windows. Her wooden desk dominated the room: green desk blotter, metal letter tray, fountain pen holder with pens sitting upright, an ink bottle and blotter. To the left, against cream-colored walls, an Olympia typewriter: rounded gray body, jutting carriage arm, and green keys.

Sister's graceful fingers trailed along the edges of an envelope, and I knew it was for me. She had read the letter, and although she had the right, I suddenly resented her touching my personal property. "About this boy who writes to you.

I removed his picture from the last letter." *Took his picture? She had no right to do that!* "You will reply and explain our policy about letters only to family." Sister John Aloysius' eyes zinged right to my heart. *Will she give it to me?* Sister handed the letter over. I did not grab. I thanked her and left the office, sad to the tips of my Dr. Scholl's shoes. In little chapel I read a harmless catalog of classes at school, of his mother and father's good health, and questions about the convent schedule. What was not in the letter was his photo.

I never inquired of a postulant or novice, "What do you write about in your letters?" Instead I stifled inquisitiveness and adopted a guarded tone in my written communication. No more requests for news and gossip, no vain talk about myself, and no more extravagant use of exclamation points. From 1962 on (except for a detailed account of the Columbus Day Storm), I kept in mind that in the convent, letters had one sole purpose: "to fulfill a filial duty, or to give edification." I monitored what I wrote to make sure that Sister John Aloysius did not have to censor my words or consider me a gossip. I created a world fit for public consumption. I didn't write about grapes planted like purple landmines in the bottom of our chocolate pudding or the novice who kept her friend awake during morning meditation by pulling her vow cord or the Irish nun who shouted in her sleep, "I will not eat that peanut butter!" I wrote my life in careful, pious strokes. "Now, there is much to be done in the name of Jesus Christ and with his power at work, I am complete."

My mother, in contrast, continued to describe tea parties and the hospital bazaar, my father's rehabilitation and her patented cellophane material, designs for playing cards and the living room renovation, a favorite book of the month (like *The Gulag Archipelago*), and her decision not to buy that toy poodle for my father. I read them and re-read them, but I could not keep them. I had a tiny community room drawer for my use and no place in the cell to store mementos or treasured sheets of paper. Besides, there was the admonition to sever family ties. I discarded my mother's letters—Thursday after Thursday, year after year. All that written vibrancy destroyed, and I don't remember grieving.

Great good, I believe, comes from the transparent heart. Years after my father's death, I traveled to Pendleton for my annual summer visit home, a gift from my Franciscan community. As usual, I slept in the extra bedroom where my mother sewed and wrote. Her Singer machine rested against one wall. The shelf next to it held Vogue and McCall dress patterns. Her desk and upright chair sat near the west wall. On the desk her pen was held upright on a marble circle, stationery beside it. South windows offered light.

Curious, I rooted through the closet and discovered my old sketch books, high school yearbooks, family photos, and a white shoe box tied with a blue ribbon. I untied the ribbon and pulled out letters addressed to my mother, the envelopes dating from 1930-1939. Settling in against the daybed pillows, I opened the letters and began to read.

My father's hand flowed smoothly across the page. His words brought him, young and earnest, into the room. In these letters he described football games and studies at the University of Oregon and his residency at the university's medical school. Sure of his love for my mother and a future of good fortune, he wrote with youth and intensity.

His words thrum with hope for a romantic, cosmopolitan life far from the woes of the Depression. He would come home to "candles, tinkling glasses," and my mother "in a soft gown that will set off the sparkle" in her eyes. He described future dinner conversations with friends, conversations laced with places he and my mother would travel: Rome and Carthage, fish streams in France, the Grand National or English Derby. He envisioned a successful life where he would not have to nickel and dime his way. He would not have to feel guilty about sending the two dollars (earned from translating German stories) as a birthday gift for his brother instead of presenting flowers to my mother. He promised her "gardenias—because there is something of you in the lily—white fragrant flowers so frail that harshness crushes them, and kindness and love seem to cause them to bloom in all their loveliness." The letters promised that he would give her the life she deserved. "I've abandoned all dreams of luxury for a great many years, but I'll give you all you need to make you happy."

Later that day, I sat down next to my mother, the letters in my hand.

She looked up. "What do you have there, Toni?"

"Letters from daddy. I found them."

Her face, full of sadness, should have stopped me, but I plunged ahead. "Listen to this: 'In a far-off tomorrow that will be here before we know it, all this lonely time of waiting will be made up for. I promise you that, dear.'"

"That was a long ago, Toni. I try not to think about it."

"Daddy hoped for so much."

My mother shook her head. "Whenever I read them, they made me cry. Now, I leave them alone."

"Would you give them to me?"

"After I die."

I put the letters carefully back into the white box, and retied the blue ribbon. These love letters would not be dismissed or destroyed. They were true keepsakes—in the fullest meaning of the word.

A few years after my mother's death, Mary wrote, "Remember mom's papers and letters? Mike and Alan have the letters they sent to her. I'll drop off yours next week."

When the box arrived, I flipped through the envelopes. My convent letters. Addresses spelling out the thirteen places I lived from 1961-1985. Inside the envelopes, I imagined detailed events from teaching assignments in California, Oregon, Washington State, and Wyoming. How had I had responded to my sister's wedding or the birth of her daughters? I couldn't wait to read of studies at Marylhurst, Gonzaga, University of Oregon, St. Bonaventure, and especially Assisi, Italy. I poured a cup of coffee, spiced it with chocolate, topped it with whipped cream, sat by the open window, and began to read.

From beginning to end, the experience was not merely disappointing, but embarrassing. I had expected vague references and pious observations from novitiate years, but not apparent disinterest in what had been happening with my family. How far removed had I been?

The letters did not improve. Why didn't I write of my nieces' Baptisms, First Communions, proms, or graduations? I didn't pen a congratulations when my mother opened her art studio. Nothing about her annual exhibit of her students' works. And for God's sake, not a word following my father's funeral in November 1975.

About myself, no mention of my marching against the Vietnam War or L'Arche retreat with Jean Vanier and his community of persons with developmental disabilities. Besides a postcard or two, no stories of my study month in Assisi. A mugging in northeast Portland and two years in a Portland skid road hotel didn't get a footnote. All those tales hidden away, as if a superior leaned over my shoulder and whispered, "No, no, Sister. You can't write that." Convent rules of open communication may have changed dramatically over the years, but I did not.

During the ten years of my father's illness, the Franciscan sisters did make sure I stayed linked to family. Visits began right after first vows in 1964. While I studied in New York, the congregation did not hesitate to pay for airplane tickets so that I could be with my dying father. Every summer, I stayed with my mother to help her out and catch up on the past year. I continued to keep secret any doubts about religious life. I did not want to admit failure or dampen my mother's pride when she said, "My daughter, the nun." Disclosure, even on cozy June evenings, had its limits.

I paid a price for guarding the word. My niece Andrea once said, "Toni, all we know about your convent life is that you entered and you left." It wasn't that I had terrible secrets requiring redaction. Omissions arose out of a habit—the paradox, not of black-and-white clothing, but pen and ink—and as a result, I robbed my family and myself of the immediate account of an incredible journey.

The convent letters hung around, like Angel's stuffed frog that needed to be discarded. No sense in letting the leg dangle by a few threads, so I either had to mend the toy or throw the thing away. I tossed the toy away and planned to do the same with the letters. First, though, I read them once more and typed out sentences that brought back memories worth holding. Gathering the rest, I bid them farewell and walked downstairs to our condo building's common shredder. Within minutes every page had whirred and rattled into skinny strips. Maybe I would look back and ask, "Why for the love of Mike, did you go and do a thing like that?" I doubt it. Unfortunately, letters scrubbed of personal experiences were never meant for a shoebox tied with a ribbon, robin's egg blue.

Prune in Season

That they, with a cheerful heart, strive to imitate
their heavenly Bridegroom, who at his birth was left
without lodging where He could rest, and who ex-
pired nude on the cross.

Most years, each of us Kennedys had possessions to call our own. My mother kept her *House Beautiful* magazines and my father, his phonograph records. Mary treasured her paper dolls, along with their wardrobes of dresses and sweaters, jackets and shoes—accompanied by little tabs to fix the fashions on the dolls. Mike had his silver jeep to ride and his ivory-handled six-shooter. Alan pedaled his red fire truck for all he was worth. My dearest treasure was Chauncey, a canary, strangely silent, until the day I played Caruso. When he heard *La donna é mobile*, my yellow songbird lifted his head, puffed out his throat, opened his beak, and trilled.

My parents were gift-givers. My father bought my mother brass: a vase, candlestick holders, a bowl, and an elephant bell. He made sure that drive-in movie nights included hot dogs, dripping with mustard, wrapped in warm paper. He bought us golf clubs and paid for country club membership, not so that he and my mother could socialize, but so that we kids could play our eighteen holes, sip lemonade on the nineteenth, and collect over a dozen trophies. My mother wrapped our birthday and Christmas presents in Hallmark's best.

Gifts, though, cost money, and as generous as my parents were, money-sense escaped them. A propensity for unwise financial choices did not appear suddenly with the arrival of children. These decisions had a longer history. Rumor was that my paternal grandfather Daniel opposed my parents' marriage, not because he disliked her, but because he believed, "What Charlie needs is a bookkeeper, not an artist." Daniel did not live to see his worries materialize, but in 1951, a nurse, who ran my father's office, embezzled funds. The medical practice he had worked to establish suffered a loss of $20,000 (close to $155,000 in today's dollars). I do not remember the quarrels or packing up our belongings or driving away from our beloved Birch Lane home, located high on a hill with woods and apple trees.

I learned early that homes, like gifts, did not last.

We moved to a rental farmhouse on the edge of Eugene. We had a cherry tree to climb, and the midnight blue Cadillac that my father had always wanted, and Chubb, a horse for Mary, but from behind closed doors we heard our parents' raised voices, though they had promised "never to quarrel in front of the children." Months later my father sat at the dining room table, holding his head. A strangled sound erupted and I thought, *That's how men sound when they cry.* One after-noon strangers loaded Chubb into a trailer. Another day, while my father sat by the window, the men arrived to repos-sess his Cadillac. The quarrels, though, did not disappear. I do not recall saying goodbye to neighbors or the move away from the rental farmhouse.

We spent months in another Eugene rental within walk-ing distance of St. Mary's elementary school. The house was a two-story, with a roof in need of repair, and a front lawn— more weed than grass. That summer, I sat by the white picket fence, waiting for the neighbor girl to walk by. She wore white T-strap sandals and I imagined wearing brand new shoes like hers. In September, I sat in a fifth-grade classroom and let Sister Stella Maris smile away my fear, but in autumn months my mother took me with her to homes with cut-glass windows and lion door knockers, and requested money owed to my father for medical bills. Some-times we left with an envelope, but most days we left with a promise. When Christmas came, I don't recall gifts or a tree, but the Holy Names sisters brought a basket with a turkey, fresh rolls and butter, cheese, and apples bright red. My fa-ther said, "We don't accept charity," and closed the door. In spring, I cradled a flashlight, digging up earthworms to sell. As I placed the squirming, pink creatures in a Folger's coffee can, I dreamed of a jar, filled to the top, with pennies.

Then we moved to a smaller space, behind the rental, and I recall a hot plate and warm buttered biscuits. My father and I visited dimly-lit, crowded pawnshops. Behind cases of glass, gold pocket watches, amethyst and emerald rings, charm bracelets, and tie clips glittered. Ceramic flower vases and snow globes, silver platters and porcelain dolls filled shelves behind the desk where the man in glasses smiled kindly. On the first visit my father brought a brass bowl and our ivory crucifix. A pain tightened in my chest at what we had to let go, but he promised that when times improved we could buy back the treasures we had hocked.

We lived, finally, in a one-bedroom motel. My father smoked and drank, raged and wept. Weekdays the four of us traveled by bus to get to school. On the bus, I argued that Santa Claus was real, and the older boys laughed, and I cried, and Michael put his arm around me and said that Santa did exist. I remember ironing my one dress—a purple one with yellow flowers. "If you are clean and neat, no one will notice that you wear your one dress," my mother told me. On weekends, Mary twirled on the swing. Mike and Alan lined up aqua swirlies and yellow opals, and flicked those marbles, straight and true. But we kids also pushed wheelbarrows of toys, books, and records across a field to an auction arena and listened to the man sing away our belongings.

Our precious items could be there one day and gone the next.

One day, Father Alan visited us. He spoke in private to my parents, and the next day, I felt a bit of the darkness lift. I remember packing the little we possessed in a small U-Haul trailer and winding our way over Route 30 and into the brown contours of Eastern Oregon, and finally arriving in Pendleton. We settled into a nice house on top of a hill, across from the Eastern Oregon State Hospital, where my father practiced medicine again. We had plenty to eat and golf to play. My parents, generous but unwise gift-givers, once again celebrated birthdays, Christmas, and Easter and paid off—month by month, year by year—the $20,000 dollars of tax debt owed to the IRS.

When God called me to the convent, I moved to a beautiful home of brick and ivy, a home that we nuns knew would last forever. Within a community of caring, dedicated sisters, we promised to imitate Christ on the cross, stripped of all material goods. Because we shared everything in common, all our needs were met. We had adequate food, clothing, and shelter. We had physicians at our disposal and education programs that I considered a rival to Smith or Bryn Mawr. The few items in my cell and the prayer books in my pew would be there day after day, without fail. Though these items did not belong to me and were only for my use, they would not disappear. God provides. Everything is gift.

Unlike my family, my Franciscan community did not give presents for birthdays or Christmas, but we did receive them. Friends and family sent fruitcakes, poppy seed bread, and boxes of Whitman and Sees chocolates. My mother sent carefully wrapped packages of cookies—chocolate chip and peanut butter—or nuts and raisins added to Chex Mix. The day she sent tulips, I wrote to tell her they opened "in front of our Lady's statue in the refectory and they welcome us at meals. We *all* want to thank you again for the flowers and for your thoughtfulness." The gifts we received, Sister John Aloysius told us, were part of the "hundredfold," our reward for giving up family and property for the sake of the Gospel. A bountiful God cares for those who sacrifice.

On a spring day in 1962, my brother Michael came to visit, with a smile and a brown package. We walked together outside, but Sister John Aloysius tagged along, asking him about his army stint in Taipei. Michael handed me the package. "For you, sis."

I turned to Sister. "May I open this?" She nodded. The gift felt light. I untied the string, unwrapped the brown paper and tissue paper. A black sweater, soft, luxurious. Mine.

He said, "I got it a size bigger so it will fit over your habit."

When I put the sweater on, it sagged a bit, and I hoped Sister hadn't noticed. "I love it, Mike."

Sister said, "Antoinette, I will take that while you say goodbye to your brother."

Removing the sweater, I placed it in Sister's hands. Michael and I walked to the front of the main house, where his green Gremlin sat parked, and I hugged him goodbye.

For the first day or two, I waited for the gift to appear in my cell. In clear disobedience to the Constitutions, I sneaked upstairs and into the linen room, opened closets, and checked shelves. I raged inside. *She had no right to take it.*

But she did. My life was the common life where no sister was allowed to keep any gift for her own personal use. The community supplied all we needed.

Six months later, I was a canonical novice with more time for theological study, prayer, and spiritual reading. One day I found a slim volume on our bookshelf entitled *Prune with Love*, the story of a vineyard worker who tends vines as black and gnarled as his heart. It was a love story and a parable: a man devotes himself to his wife and his land, their faithfulness to one another endures, and the land flourishes. When he loses his wife, he leaves everything behind and wanders, crushed by sadness, raging at God. What redeems him are the vines he tends with love.

The book's theme presented a choice: continue being unhappy with life as it is, or whittle away old desires, one knife flick, then another. Sometimes when I thought of the sweater warming the wider shoulders of a nun, my agitation surfaced. I asked myself, *How long would I hang on to this seeming slight?* Only with a pure heart, detached and free, could I bring myself to the altar of God the following year and pledge my vow of poverty. The sweater was not stolen from me. It was not sold at an auction. In my life as a nun—a life I had freely chosen—the sweater was never really mine.

As months passed, I found contentment in having little. With my family, I had feared doing without the shiny apple or the T-strap sandals, as though the deprivations would cripple me or lessen my worth. In sharing what I had with my sisters and working for the common good, a freedom blossomed within me, a belief that I could travel unencumbered. Both hands empty and lifted to God became my image of poverty.

During the winter of my second-year novitiate, my parents sent a Christmas gift with a card addressed "to all the postulants and novices." Sister John Aloysius opened the bulky present during the huge snowfall that blanketed Palatine Hill and all Portland. Sleds. The perfect gift. In my letter home, I described us nuns, standing outside, stomping our feet to keep warm, tossing holy water to christen "St. Christopher" and "Michael the Archangel," and the exuberant rides down the sloping lawn. I closed the letter with gratitude to them for sending a gift that everyone could enjoy.

With the other nuns, I sledded down the hill, bursting with pride and happiness. The sleds brought back memories of winters on Birch Lane, of snow and boots and tomato soup and toasted cheese sandwiches—when money problems did not sap my parents' energy; when I was sure the little red wagon and hobby horses would never leave us. The sleds would last—no one would nibble them away and no one would remove them, like wilting flowers or a black sweater. Once snow fell, the novices, throughout the years, would pull them from storage. Christopher and Michael were blessed members of the Franciscan family, ready for anyone who wanted to slide down the marshmallow lawn of Palatine Hill—our home forever.

In late November of 1975, I flew from St. Bonaventure University in New York, westward toward Portland, traveled eastward by bus to Pendleton, and arrived at the hospital where my father was dying. I should have been prepared for death's inexorable pruning. After all, my studies at the time had focused on 1500 pages of Franciscan medieval documents, replete with stories and the words of St. Francis, the poor one, the *Poverello*: in imitation of the crucified Savior, he stripped himself of family, property, and health. I forgot his tale of perfect poverty as I waited in that room. True to my core flaw—the belief that I could change what was, I tripped once again, saddened by what I had not witnessed. I missed the surgery that opened my father's cancer-riddled body. I missed the doctors' sigh as they closed him up again.

With my family, I did see the nurses making his last hours comfortable with lotion massage and morphine doses every four hours. I did see his pale body on the hospital bed. My father had been whittled clean: his elegance, his classic verbal wit, the timbre of his magnificent speaking voice, and his ability to stride in joy and anger over any road or stream of his choice. He ended his journey in pain and humiliation, shuffling, then crawling half-way up that high green hill. Never got to Ireland. Never claimed his castle. Never realized the dreams he wrote in letters to my mother. His last words were not a cry for forgiveness, but a statement of fact: "I've suffered enough. I'm getting out of here," and his weary body slipped into a coma.

I thought, *Dad found the ultimate escape from worry.*

My mother, though, knew his escape was only partial. "Hearing is the last sense to go. Take time with your father. Tell him how much you love him." When my turn came, I held his hand—still beautiful even with the pale-yellow nicotine stains on his thumb and forefinger. With my family, I sang "Danny Boy" and laughed as Alan recalled one of our father's favorites, the epitaph joke, "I expected this. But not so soon." Ready or not, my father's life narrowed to strips of blinds, sheets, tubes, and a bed. Snow drifted into the darkness outside. One last exhalation and he was gone.

After my father's death, still in mourning, and inspired by the material poverty of St. Francis of Assisi, I struggled to understand the abundance we had as nuns and the destitution of those in the world. How did the vow reconcile any downward spiral, like the one my family suffered—from the top of Birch Lane to a motel on the outskirts of town? How did we, as nuns, see a blessing in unrealized dreams and a child's small cache of pennies?

As vocation director and teacher to the postulants and novices, I assumed the role of prophet, questioning our comfortable lifestyle. Instead of listening to others with diverse viewpoints, I railed against what I deemed excess and prided myself on keeping my clothes and mementos to a minimum. Once, a sister stood at the threshold of my bedroom and said, "Why does your place always look like you are moving out?" I saw this question as an affirmation. I took it upon myself, in ways subtle and overt, to criticize how we nuns lived the vow of poverty. While I placed judgment on the sisters with whom I lived, the congregation, true to its commitment to each of us, faithfully continued to feed, clothe, shelter, and educate me.

There resided the irony. All I had to do at age eighteen was accept the sacrifice of God's call, and the hundredfold was guaranteed. By pledging poverty, I sidestepped money problems. In having nothing that belonged to me, I had everything I needed, especially a mansion for a home. This paradox could have been a reason for delighting in God's wondrous providence. Instead, after too many years of receiving gifts freely given, I made another choice. Once I

knew I could make it on my own financially, I sought another escape—this time from a religious family who had
promised me security until death.

In the year 2000, the Sisters of St. Francis decided to sell
Our Lady of Angels Convent. As much as they wanted to
keep their property, the maintenance had become too great
an expense. The sisters invited former nuns, families, clergy, and friends to come together for a farewell liturgy. Main
chapel remained beautiful as ever, with its sweeping arc of
altar rail and pillar; its wood statues of Mary and Joseph and
the crucified Christ suspended above the sanctuary. The autumn sun shone through the stained glass and painted the
marble walls. Jubilation may have risen from the harmony
and readings, but we all knew it was a day of deep sorrow.
After Mass we nuns and former nuns walked the grounds
and along the cloister walk of this beautiful place that had
been our home. Each of us, whether still in religious life or
not, held memories we did not want to relinquish: autumns
of rain and vibrant leaves, winters of snow and Christmas,
springs of blossoms and azalea buds, summers of softball
and starlit nights. And always the music. We said goodbye to
our precious home located high on a hill with its woods and
orchard of apples and cherries. Prune with love. Nothing
lasts forever.

How to dwell in holy detachment still confounds me.
Jesus in the Gospels, St. Francis in his writings, and a journey unencumbered still attract me. Yet, I refuse to relinquish
my treasures: a Vermeer print of *Girl Reading a Letter by an*

Open Window, my father's brass elephant bell, a wood rosary from Bethlehem, my dulcimer, and my pen-and-ink drawing. I am possessive of my books: my father's 1895 Tennyson and Longfellow volumes, Makine's *Music of a Life*, Guardini's *The Living God*, Gallico's *The Snow Goose*, Thomas' *A Child's Christmas in Wales*, *Franciscan Morning and Evening Praise*, and Bible. I love my sweaters, although Michael's alpaca wool cardigan from a Taipei shop has never been among them. And, not least, my sweet Angel, whose unconditional love belongs solely to me.

On a late winter day in 2015, as Angel and I walked through Portland State's campus, I stopped to observe a young man dressed in woolen shirt, overalls, and sturdy boots. He held a long-bladed tool and stood, silent and attentive, in front of a ten-foot maple. Around the young man rushed the world: students on their way to class, the couple who ran daily with their Irish setter, the ever-present, squawking crows, and an idling Coca-Cola truck. The young man did not turn his head. His focus stayed on the tree. Slowly, he lifted the long shears, moved a step or two, and clipped off a small branch. The ritual continued: watch, wait, and clip. Little by little the tree took on clean lines.

The ritual in the park signals that before long, I'll need to surrender more than treasured possessions. I imagine death, my final escape, will not be according to plan, but will catch me off-guard, and I will sputter that it's not the right moment. I hope, though, that the specter does not resemble Albrecht Durer's skeletal Death sidling alongside on a boney steed. I'd rather he look like this focused landscaper, boots scuffed and shears in hand. Ready or not, here he comes. Watch. Wait. Clip.

Preserve This Treasure

That they put themselves under the obligation of celibacy, and bind themselves to refrain from every act whatsoever against chastity.

O n a clear autumn day in 1961, I had finished folding towels in the kitchen and was heading out the back door when the milk-delivery driver hopped out of his truck. Sandy-haired, with freckles and a wide grin, he called out, "You must be one of the new ones."

"I am," I answered, happy that this cute guy stopped to talk with me—quite a change from nothing but nuns. He asked me where I'd come from and when I told him Eastern Oregon, we talked about wheat crops and the inevitable icy roads in the Gorge. I learned he had a wife and two kids and liked his job.

"Hope to see you again," he said, and turned to pull out the trays of milk bottles.

"Me, too."

I skipped down the cloister walk.

That afternoon, Sister called me into her office and spoke briefly. "Antoinette, one of the kitchen sisters saw you conversing with the milk-delivery man." She tapped her fingers on the desk. "He needs to be about his business and you need to be about yours."

"Yes, Sister," I said.

I may have suffered irritation with the sister who snitched on me, but this incident was a beginning lesson on how to preserve the treasure that is chastity.

One of the scripture passages Sister John Aloysius used for our edification and instruction was that of the ten virgins, five of them foolish and five of them wise. Carrying lamps, they went out to meet the bridegroom and bride; but when the oil ran out, only five of them had brought extra oil, and thus only the wise virgins greeted the bridegroom and celebrated in the grand hall. With her bifocals pushed down on her nose, Sister looked at us over the rim of her glasses and quoted the line from Scripture: "Watch ye, therefore, because you know not the day nor the hour." Stay alert, Franciscan virgins, for the Divine Bridegroom is coming.

Preserve chastity through caution, she advised. Remember the words of the Rule: "the sisters must be frugal and temperate in the use of food and drink; exterior actions must be so guarded as to avoid all occasions and dangers which captivate the senses." Education in the 1950s, whether in school or home, usually did not include courses on human sexuality. There were a few exceptions. In grade school, the visiting priest demonstrated intercourse by holding a plug in one hand and socket in the other. Jabbing the two together, he said, "When the man and woman have intercourse, they both get a kind of shock."

I was appalled. After school, I headed home and around to the backyard where my mother was hanging laundry, white sheets billowing around her, a clothes pin in her hand. When I related what the priest had said, I asked, "You and daddy don't do that, do you?"

She pulled a sheet from the tub and handed me an end. Her eyes twinkled. "Well, yes, we do, Toni." She smiled. "And it's quite nice."

I swallowed hard, substituting the image of electrical equipment with my parents' embrace.

My culture—a gentler and more naïve time—pre-dated the sexual revolution. *Seventeen Magazine* told me how to dress, treat my siblings, set my hair, flirt innocently, and be a good friend. The slow dance warmed me and the kiss made me tingle, but fear of "getting into trouble" or worst of all, shaming my parents, kept me on my guard. So did the Pendleton girl who suddenly left town for six months.

We nuns maintained our innocence by refraining from gluttony and laziness and by not conversing with outsiders, even the friendly milkman. As members of a religious order, there was no need to converse with men, for by entering the convent, dating was, of course, forbidden, and marriage no longer a choice. For the time being, that was fine with me. During high school, I may have daydreamed about romance, but from my own family and families of friends, I knew that marriage ballooned into pregnancy, money fights, and housework—the washboard, ironing board, and stove. If my husband lost his job or a child broke a leg, I would have to add to my house-cleaning burden and get an outside job selling saddles and leather chaps at Hamley's. I wanted more.

By joining the Franciscans, I saw myself as part of a long tradition of innovative, adventuresome women who composed music, like Hildegard of Bingen; advised clerics, like Teresa of Avila; and ministered on foreign lands, like Mother Marianne Cope who served the Molokai lepers and cared for the dying Father Damien. Sister John Aloysius encouraged us, though, to turn to Mary, Christ's mother, as the wisest woman of all. She was young, a virgin, and the handmaid of the Lord. I had never prayed to Mary much, outside the occasional rosary, but when Sister told us to search for her in Scripture, I thought I would give Christ's mother a second chance.

As a new postulant, longing for inspiration, I found in Mary only sadness. Pregnant without a husband, she gave birth away from family. The twelve-year-old Jesus disappeared for three days without thinking how worried she must have been. As an adult, He scolded Mary for asking Him to replenish Cana's wedding wine. And at the crucifixion Christ handed her, His broken-hearted mother, over to John. Not once did Jesus call her by name or acknowledge Himself as her son. No matter how theologians justified the passages, I knew that Mary must have been very lonely.

Loneliness in the midst of thirty other souls seemed a shameful feeling to have to admit, but there it was, a hard lump in my chest, made heavier by the homesickness I tried to deny. And that is the hurt I carried when my mother came to visit. After Christmas, we sat in the blue parlor, that gracious room in the main house, across from the library with its gorgeous wood shelves and leather chairs. Victorian chairs in blue brocade matched the sofa, and windows faced the cascading lawn. A nun brought in a tray of tea and cookies.

My mother smiled. "Thank you, Sister."

The sister set the plate on the polished coffee table. "'Tis lovely to see you, Mrs. Kennedy."

My mother's gray hair curled slightly around her cheekbones. Pearl clip-on earrings and necklace, beige knit dress and tan gloves made her appearance all of a piece. She slanted her legs to one side so that the tips of her brown and white spectator pumps touched the carpet.

The sister left us, mother and daughter sitting together.

"You are happy here, aren't you, Toni?"

I thought of the Christmas celebrations and the music, the safety and sisterhood of the convent, but deep down was that discontent. "It isn't exactly what I expected."

"Life never is, sweetheart." She sighed. "How like your father you are."

From a place so unacknowledged that my stomach turned, a desire arose: to go home with her. How would I do that? Tell her now and watch her face fill with disappointment?

She was the parent most proud of my decision. Yet I missed so much about home: my brother Alan, his wry sense of humor and his steadiness; my boyfriend and slumber parties with best friends; my mother promising, "This that I worried about yesterday has happened today and is nothing";

my father appearing in my doorway before dawn. I ached to say to my mother, Take me with you. Instead, I said, "I'm really lonely."

My mother's hands enclosed mine. "Loneliness is part of life. There are times, even when you children are around me and your father is close, when I feel alone." My mother touched my cheek. "This is our yearning for God and for heaven." Lines like sketch marks around her eyes and mouth reminded me that she had enough worries.

For the rest of the visit, I didn't complain. We walked hand-in-hand on the cloister walk and out into the circular drive. As she opened the car door, she smiled. "This, too, shall pass, Toni." I did not climb into the pink Mercury. I waved goodbye.

In lessons and by her example, Sister John Aloysius encouraged us to preserve the treasure of chastity through community. Once again, she found an apt directive from the Rule: "They shall manifest to each other signs of a true and holy friendship. Let each one, in a spirit of humility, believe herself the servant of all the others."

Just as my mother had promised, my loneliness did pass. Gradually, I began to appreciate the sisters with whom I lived. Thirty of us, all young, idealistic, in love with God, coming from the Pacific Northwest, California, and the Irish Republic worked, prayed, played, and studied together. No doubt our life was blessed through the close-knit community of friends, and as Sister reminded us, one more proof of God's hundredfold.

But Sister added a caveat. Community is not for the self-ish, or the indulgent, or a substitute for God's love. Relationships need to free the individual sister, not lay claim to her. Our rooms were not visiting places—ever. Our cells had three purposes: silence, prayer, and sleep. Sister continued the sessions on chastity with further warnings about the dangers of liking one another too much and to avoid "all that savors of particular friendship." Commitment to community is to be marked by a universal affection for all—a love untainted by favoritism.

As I listened to her, I took a hard look at myself. In high school, I ran with the popular crowd, made friends with upper classmen, and had three best friends. If our senior year separated us because of boyfriends, family troubles, and decisions about the future, our first three high school years were a period of constant togetherness on the school steps for lunch, in the gymnasium, cheering at ball games, on the stage in Catholic Youth Organization plays, and on the phone. We were the keen group sharing private stories and laughing at inside jokes.

Through Sister's novitiate instructions, I saw my high school friendships in a new light. We were particular friends. We were a clique in a very small class in a very small school. To think of the other girls standing on the outside, waiting for an invitation that never arrived, made me feel ashamed. Did they face loneliness most school days? My friends and I were not mean or vindictive, simply an exclusive, closed circle.

Sister John Aloysius invited us to reflect on past behavior and to live differently. Love others equally by seeing beyond our initial rejection of the sister whose interests we don't appreciate, or the sister who irritates, or the nun who dislikes us. Luke's Gospel repeated Sister's admonition: "For if you love those who love you, what credit is that to you? Even sinners love those who love them." I made a promise: no favoritism, but instead try to strengthen the bonds of the entire community. My singular and particular love belongs to God alone.

Sister's instructions appeared in concrete form during the two summers of my novitiate. From June to August, The Hill welcomed nuns on summer break from missions in Washington, Oregon, California, and Wyoming. Sisters, separated during the year, walked on the grounds in pairs or small groups, played soft ball, shot baskets, played cards, baked cookies, and weeded the rose gardens. No superior stopped them or clucked in disapproval and I thought how nice it would be to have a best friend. I imagined the two of us riding a jeep in Antigua, playing jump rope with orphans in Spokane, or having a picnic on Palatine Hill's lawn.

Some nuns spent the summer sitting on the sidelines. Maybe they didn't care and wanted to be alone. Of course, at the end of summer, the nuns with friends and those who had seemed left out faced a similar separation. When they packed their bags to go back to mission, did they feel sad at saying goodbye? As I watched the cars drive away, I wondered if any of them, once they started teaching again, would experience loneliness—the ache that my mother said was part of life. Chastity meant you could have time with friends, but sooner or later, the time ended.

As fun as it was to watch the sisters come together and to imagine my own best friend at some future date, the sisters who inspired me most were the ones whose love seemed unconditional. One sister especially stands out. Every summer when she came from her mission assignment and arrived at The Hill, she filled the space around her with what seemed like an aura of light. Beautiful within and without (what we then called the "Black Irish"), she stayed attentive, gentle, and kind. If she had been one of those virgins who waited for the bridegroom's arrival, and if one of the others had forgotten lamp oil, Sister would have said, in her soft brogue, "Here, take mine." Watching her genuine goodness and joy made me realize how love eased loneliness. Sister lived chastity by being a true friend to all.

Yet, temperamentally I was light years from her holiness, although, during the months leading into canonical year, I practiced becoming less self-preoccupied and more alert to the needs of others. What did not come easily was gentleness—always there was life as it was and life as I wanted it to be. Battling with my need to shape situations was the admonition "not to give occasion of annoyance to others, although they think they have just cause for doing so." Too much my father's daughter, I could be unpredictably angry if my opinion was not heeded, if my schedule was interrupted, or if I did not get enough time alone.

What saved me from explosions were the novitiate's clear boundaries. Times of silence let me seethe within instead of striking out verbally. The more I practiced acts of kindness, the more I thought I had my explosive nature under control.

Month by month, I believed I was becoming the chaste, wise virgin.

The most important way to preserve the treasure of chastity, Sister John Aloysius told us—once again referring to the Rule—was to "put no trust in our own strength, but be continually engaged in prayer." During the last two years of the novitiate, Sister focused her lessons on instilling within us the desire for contemplation. She taught by word and example that we would keep our chastity vow if we fostered an intimate relationship with God. "God is the More that we seek," she said. "The Infinite God is your Bridegroom. Belong to Him alone." Again, she noted the great women: St. Theresa, the Little Flower and St. Clare, friend of Francis, women whose biographies declared them spouses of Christ.

Although the "sweet espousal" approach didn't work for me, contemplative prayer did. As a child, worried about my parents or angry with a playmate, I climbed high in the cherry tree, and there, among the leaves, found peace. As a nun, contemplation became my new hiding space. I searched for passages where Christ escaped the crowds, where David's music soothed Saul, where God told Abram to look at a star-studded sky, and where, anytime I wanted, I could rest in God's open palm. And I slipped into my meditation book the poetry of Gerard Manley Hopkins and T.S. Eliot, A.E. Housman and Daniel Berrigan.

Contemplation, Sister told us, was hard work. We nuns were given help in getting rid of pesky distractions. Imagine a box and toss them in, one at a time. Pray that God remove worldly thoughts. Although I listened carefully, soon enough

I discovered how easily prayer came to me. I wasn't perfect yet—resentment against the sister who burned the toast, impatience for the nun who mispronounced "epitome," and loneliness that sometimes snaked into my heart may have pricked me. Yet, when I closed my eyes in prayer, God welcomed me into tranquil Presence. Just like that. Without knowing it, my mother had, long ago, turned me into a contemplative when she first said, "Take time for yourself."

For three years I learned what it meant to be a good nun, all in preparation for the time I would kneel before my community and declare the vow of chastity. A deeper reality than visiting with a milkman, a wider truth than loneliness, and higher desire than any sexual needs, chastity relied on sisterhood. Together, holding lamps aloft, we would thread our way through the narrow gate.

When I read the story of the ten virgins now, I find something humorous and fully human about the women who don't plan ahead and the supposedly wise ones who refuse to share. Of course, the wedding doors are shut on the unprepared.

Rather than a lesson on how to live attentively, the parable seems more a celebration of human frailty and the Gospel story a little summary of my own journey. At times ultra-prepared and other times dreamily out-of-touch, I have done my share of refusing kindness and pounding on doors, demanding to be part of the celebration.

While I no longer live in religious life, I do believe in chastity, or what we now call celibacy. People sublimate sexual desires with service to the poor and marginalized; they give up marriage and intimacy to care for a parent or disabled sibling. Others choose chastity because their passion is research or the literary life or wild mustangs or trafficked human beings. Some have never found the right partner. Of the nuns and priests who have inspired me, most of them have remained in religious life and have continued to live chastity with humility and integrity.

I was never meant to live this vow, not because of the sublimation of sexual desires, but because of the commitment to community life. Away from novitiate boundaries of silence and prayer, removed from my idealistic, young companions, caught up in the time-crunch of lesson plans and mission responsibilities, I gradually reverted to old ways of irritation and harsh judgment. Times of contemplation shrank. Emotionally, I withdrew from the sisterhood that is integral to living chastity. Worse, the longer I remained in the Franciscans, the more toxic my responses became. No surprise that when I left the convent, few nuns wrote to wish me well or to express sorrow at my departure.

At first, whenever colleagues or friends asked why I never married, I joked about avoiding the bar scene or the impossibility of finding the perfect man. A more honest response is not only my fear of entrapment, but my inability to take people and situations just as they are, free of my judgment and criticism. Those who love me tease, "Toni, marriage would never have worked for you." True enough. I'm a reliable listener, able to empathize, but there is another, less hospitable side. When events do not unfold as I judge they ought to, my anger surfaces. On good days, my husband and I would have spent wild and wonderful moments together, but on bad days he would regret not having relegated me to a cottage of my own. And the children? As adults, they would know that a visit would include a favorite meal and good conversation, but God help them if they brought an iPhone to the table. I have changed little from the woman who desired to travel unencumbered, disappointed with the past, discontented with the present, and expecting the perfect. Years ago, Father Hayes had said to me, "Only God will satisfy you." He was right.

My tranquil self recognizes a need for others and thus, I do not live alone, but share community with another ex-nun, the Franciscan sister who first invited me to live among the poor and with whom I lived at the Rich Hotel in Portland. Even though we have Eastern Oregon roots, Catholicism, and the Franciscan order in common and share a love for animals, the intellectual life, and justice, life has not always been as peaceful as it is now. Marge admits how difficult it was to live with my anger that could be "unpredictable and explosive." Over the years, though, her friendship has helped mellow me. We are sisters, keeping our circle of community inclusive and our home open to others.

When human companionship is not enough, I find solace in a dog. For thirty years I have had them—shelter mutts except for my Shih Tzu. Ten years ago, I had expected to pick her up from a farmhouse surrounded with fencing and a yard full of grubby pups, but I was in for a surprise. Around the curve of a private drive, a one-story house of stone and wood sat, regally perched on the top of a hill. Inside, and separated by a guard rail, a canine palace appeared: dining room, tiled floor, kitchen, nook, sofas, chairs, beds. Floor to ceiling windows gave the animals a view of the Sandy River and mountains.

In a large open crate quivered two puppies, tails high and wagging. Immediately the auburn, boisterous one, pawed at the crate. The other, white and quiet, leaned forward, her eyes like ink pools, and lifted her chrysanthemum face. She woofed, "You are mine." Miracle of miracles, her birthday is October 2, Feast of the Guardian Angels. Naming her Cherubima or Seraphina was never an option. She is Angel, my *Heilige Schutzengel*, a fluffy, funny pledge of God's unconditional particular friendship.

I cannot escape the child I once was and the religious life I once lived. Quiet places and contemplation continue to calm my anger, and loneliness still hangs around the edges of my life in community. One morning, Angel and I sat on the patio, both of us listening to water flow against agates in a small fountain and both of us peaceful. As my little guardian reclined on her back, paws up, defenseless, I figured it was a good thing no attacker was in sight. Turning my new Chekhov coffee cup, I enjoyed the collage of his terse wisdom regarding talent and knowledge, faith and science, trust and belief. If Angel were sitting in the chair opposite so that we could visit, she would see this quotation, "Money, like vodka, turns a person into an eccentric." The words facing me warn, "If you are afraid of loneliness, do not marry."

I swear I can hear my mother's spirit brushing against the bubbling fountain. *What did I tell you?*

Lift Your Wings

That they bear in mind that by making the Vow of Obedience, they have renounced their own will, in order to obey the will of the superior.

The Bible story of Moses describes him holding aloft stone tablets emblazoned with the Ten Commandments. Clouds roll, thunder bellows, and lightning cracks the darkness—signs that these laws come directly from an almighty author. The commandments proclaim the essentials of holiness: God alone is worthy of worship; Sunday is a holy day; parents and legitimate authority must be obeyed; no lying, stealing, or slander; and no coveting what others possess.

To strengthen the commandments, Catholics in the 1940s and 1950s had the additional *Baltimore Catechism*. The book, filled with questions and answers, made clear that Adam and Eve passed their disobedience to us. An accompanying illustration reinforced the seriousness of their sin.

The soul was like a milk bottle. Without sin, the milk was pure. With sin, the liquid turned splotchy. The black bottle described mortal sin and separation from God's presence. Any act of disobedience stained the soul. Disobedience made God unhappy.

Yet I was not an obedient child. As kids, we played a game called, "Mother, May I" on the gravel playground behind the grade school. One of the children got to be mother and the rest of us played the children who pretended to mind her. The mother would face away from us. Taking turns, we asked if we could take three steps or leap backwards, each question prefaced by "Mother, may I?" The mother could say "no" and declare what we *could* do or say "yes" to our request. The goal was to jump, step, or slither forward into the mother position. Early in the game, I'd slip away and swing from the monkey bars rather than wait around to ask permission.

In God's powerful sight I spent my childhood, and God was everywhere. God smiled when I let our spaniel Penny have her puppies on my bed. God frowned when I quarreled with my brother and slammed the bedroom door. God nodded as I decorated the statue of the Virgin Mary with tissue paper roses. God wept when I mocked our school principal. God nodded in agreement when, as a seventh grader, I asked my parents for a canary.

Named after the Irish-American tenor, Chauncey Olcott was my pet and my responsibility. I fed him, bundled up the dirty newspaper in his cage, replaced his seed and water, and turned on Caruso while he swung on his perch and chirped along. When I opened the door and extended my finger, the canary hopped right on. As the days passed, I grew to hate the cage.

"It's so small," I complained.

My mother warned me. "Toni, don't you dare let that bird out. Anything could happen to him."

My father said. "Chauncey needs to stay put." He whistled for the dog. "Unless you want Cookie to make short work of him."

"Okay," I said, but that wasn't really a promise.

One day, left on my own, I let the dog out in the back yard, hurried into the living room, and opened Chauncey's cage. His licorice eyes stared back and his pink beak opened in a smile. He hopped into my hand, his orange claws tickling my palm. Slowly, I carried him out. Hesitant at first, Chauncey looked around, and then suddenly spread his wings, and flew from couch to piano keys to lamp shade to book shelf and back again to my finger. Thus began our freedom ritual. Even though God clucked in disapproval, the bird's freedom felt like a blessing. He would fly around, return, and soar off again, only to come back to me, sometimes perched on my shoulder, twittering, his feathers ruffled, and his heart beating rapidly with what I thought was pure bliss.

Months later, I removed Chauncey's cover and found him, motionless, at the bottom of his cage. I reached in and carefully touched him, all the while whispering his name. No little chirp, no heartbeat. My stomach knotted. My parents had told me to keep the bird safe and sound in his cage. By disobeying, I had worn down his tiny heart.

I cried and begged God to forgive me. I buried Chauncey with ceremony, digging a deep hole in the earth outside my bedroom window. I asked my father for two tongue depressors to make a cross for his grave and placed wildflowers beside it. I prayed for my canary and carried a burden of nagging guilt. If I hadn't let him fly free, Chauncey would be alive. I never confessed my sin to a priest, but lived with an inky splotch on my soul. I carried, like Eve, the curse of disobedience.

God continued to watch me through the rest of junior high and into high school. The all-seeing Deity was not simply an observer, but a God with a plan. This blueprint we Catholics called God's will. God arranged our future. In trying to discover what God wanted, I looked for heroes. Damien lived with the Molokai lepers. Dr. Tom Dooley helped the sick of Laos, so I read his memoirs: *Deliver Us from Evil*, *The Edge of Tomorrow*, and *The Night They Burned the Mountain*. How happily God observed these men who served Him. By the time I was a senior, I understood exactly why the nun would say, "Toni, if God is calling you, and you refuse, you'll never be happy." First and foremost, be obedient to the Will of God.

Readiness to obey was key to life at Our Lady of Angels Convent. From the outset, God's plan demanded that we manifest an obedience that is "blind, childlike, and prompt." I had never liked the playground game of "Mother, May I," and here I was again, but in the grown-up version. An eye-opening lesson took shape following the arrival of the postulant Pauline. I may have been a few hours late on Entrance Day, but Pauline arrived two weeks late. No emergency caused this delay. She arranged her entrance to the convent so that she could attend the annual September celebration called the Pendleton Round-Up. The rest of us postulants may have been obedient to the rules, but she'd had more fun—and all in God's sight. The Almighty observed her as she ate hamburgers and partied with family and friends during the Happy Canyon Indian pageant. No lightning struck her. God looked upon her action, certainly, but left her alone.

Pauline strode through the novitiate with freedom and energy. She stood equal in height to Sister John Aloysius and teased her. A mention of her late entrance and Pauline laughed: "Now, John," (no one addressed Sister John Aloysius that way), nothing could be *that* important." And she made Sister laugh. With good humor, Pauline waved away the immutability of God's design. Before November rains struck, Pauline the postulant was gone. We did not get to tell her goodbye. God was all-knowing, but we postulants did not possess that power. Silence kept us from inquiring on the status of one another. Pauline left no announcement or letter tacked to a bulletin board, but did leave the curtain drawn back from her cleared-out cell and an empty chair at meals and recreation. She must have ambled out the front entrance, exiting as she had entered: on her own terms. I was pretty sure Sister John Aloysius missed her as much as I did.

Life moved on for the rest of us postulants, living within the sight of God and that of our novice mistress. Novices told us that Sister not only had eyes in the back of her head, but she had a sixth sense. "Watch out," they'd tease. "She'll appear when you least expect her." Laughter accompanied the warning. I watched these young novices, at ease and unafraid of Sister. Would I ever be that free?

Sister John Aloysius warned us that the most difficult gift we could give God was not our poverty or our chastity, but our will. Even the slightest desire to have our own way kept us bound and separated from God, like a bird caught in a slender thread or tied by a thick cord. Sister's instructions on threads and birds did not solve my dilemma. Whether snared by our own will or that of the vow, we were still trapped. Month by month, I tried to push aside a desire to break free and prayed for the grace to release my will, conscious that actions took place in God's sight and under Sister's watchful eye.

No questioning, no hesitation was permitted—whether in simple commands to rise at the first ring of the bell or decide what job I would do for the rest of my life. Early in the first semester of my canonical year, Sister Joan, not only director of education, but also of mission activities, sent word that she wanted to see me. Up the winding staircase of the main house I climbed, down the narrow hallway, and into her office. Her smiling, ruddy face (made smaller by the cap and veil) welcomed me. She sat behind a large mahogany desk, windows open behind her, leafy trees shifting the light.

Sister Joan spoke of my future work in the community; how, since my father was a doctor, I might consider nursing. Her suggestion recalled his words. "The medical profession treats nurses like second-class citizens. You'll end up carrying bed pans. No daughter of mine will be a nurse." My father, the physician, friend of nurses, knew their predicament. I believed him and mentally crossed that career off my list.

While sitting in Sister's spacious office, I did not mention that my heroes were Tom Dooley, Damien of Molokai, or the Maryknoll Missionaries. I did not beg to be sent to our mission in Puerto Rico. In no way did I reveal my keen dislike for the classroom. God watched. I could not fail this test of obedience. The cage door shut. I would not be careening in a jeep in the jungle, but instead I would be teaching, not in high school in the green Pacific Northwest, but in some grade school in sun-dried California. I nodded and smiled, so proud of myself for what I did not express. God must have been very pleased.

Good thing for me was that being stuck in a classroom wouldn't happen for another year and a half. By that time, I thought maybe Sister Joan might forget about our meeting and she would call me to her office once again. Then, I could tell her about my hopes to become a missionary, or better yet, instead of enduring teacher certification classes, I could take art lessons. When, caught in the real world, I felt the will of God trapping me, I imitated Scarlet O'Hara and told myself I would think about it tomorrow. In times of reflection and quiet prayer, I admitted to myself that I was nowhere near being ready to promise obedience.

On a late summer day in 1963, just before entering my second year as a novice, I happened upon a slim volume written by Romano Guardini entitled *The Living God.* His theology opened a door. God's will was not a fixed

blueprint, but what ought to result from work and free choices. Partners with the Lord of the Universe, our footsteps left
a mark. God does not trip us as we escape with stolen plums
or strike us when we open a bird cage. This God, Guardini
taught, was the God who stepped out on the firmament and
called all creation "Good."

As I stopped equating obedience with subservience,
God's will and God's vision no longer threatened my freedom, and sure enough, my relationship with Sister John Aloysius changed. I began to appreciate her sly wit and spiritual
clarity; she was no longer the stern taskmaster or a dreaded
leader ready to call out, "No, you may not." I teased the postulants about Sister appearing when they least expected it.
In December, listening to *A Child's Christmas in Wales*, I, too,
laughed at Dylan Thomas' version of disobedience: neighbor
boys had been told not to skate on the pond. But they did.
And they drowned. Cause and effect.

With my second year as a novice coming to a close, and
first profession looming, Sister John Aloysius did not su-
garcoat what an obedient life might resemble. No question
that we would commit to a hierarchical system of superiors and subjects. As Franciscans, we must be "most careful
not to murmur against the commands of the Superior, even
if these were given with indiscretion and imprudence," but
must cheerfully submit. While Sister lectured, I felt old fears
surface. What if gentle Sister Joan assigned me to a school
where the children only spoke Spanish? What if I had to
teach percentages or music theory? What if I said, "No, I
will not do that?" Worrying about the future didn't count. I

would go where I was sent and do what I was told. I thought of my poor, dead Chauncey at the bottom of his cage, and promised myself that I would be true to the vow of obedience. I would not choose my own will.

The closer profession appeared on the horizon, the less we were mere fledglings who would leave the nest and make room for the next batch. Instead, we would be equals with this formidable woman who would no longer be our novice mistress, but our friend and sister. All of us would be Franciscans, not children on a playground looking to sneak out of the game, but adults who freely chose to submit to authority with humility and simplicity.

Instead of walking away from Our Lady of Angels—every step in the sight of God—I wrote a formal letter stating my intention to stay; in my will, I signed away the right to goods and money that might come to me later; I knelt before the provincial council and asked, "Mother, may I continue in this life?" I entered into a silent ten-day retreat. Perhaps my spiritual director said, "Are you sure, Sister Miriam Michael?" What I recall most clearly was the impetus to move forward. *I can always change my mind –six more years until final vows.* Even though doubts surfaced, I did not want to be left behind.

Profession day arrived. The organ announced our entrance, the choir sang, the bishop, provincial and general minister of the entire order watched while we received the black veil and crucifix of the professed sister. I knelt at the altar railing, held the lit candle and declared my desire to follow God's holy will:

*I, Sister Miriam Michael, make unto Almighty
God, in presence of the Blessed Virgin Mary, Mother
of God, of our Holy Father, St. Francis, of all the
Saints, and before you, Reverend Mother Mary Ag-
nes, Superior General of Sisters known as the Philadelphia Foundation of the Third Order of St. Francis, the promise and vow to observe Poverty, Chastity,
and Obedience, for the space of one year in the said
Congregation of the Third Order of St. Francis; and
I propose to live in the same according to the Constitutions approved by the Holy See.*

As I finished saying my vows, this thought erupted: *If I got
through the novitiate, I can get through anything.* Afterward, in
the refectory, I stood with my set. We blessed the food and
turned over the plate in front of us—like newly professed
Franciscans had done for eons. On a strip of paper was my
first mission assignment: Our Lady of Perpetual Help Grade
School, Riverside, California. There it was in print; no chance
to ask for a do-over or a mulligan.

I cannot recall a sense of God's will drawing me into the
heat of Southern California. But I did imagine Sister Joan,
not God, designing my future. She sat in front of a giant chart
made up of little houses. A bowl held the photo of each sister. Reaching into the bowl, Sister arranged and rearranged
who would go where. One sister would be in a new place.
Another would return to the mission she had left. Hours later, Sister had the houses filled, each nun secured in a preordained niche. Thus, the sisters—including us, the six newly

professed—received their assignments by virtue of holy obedience.

Leave it to the Brothers Grimm to inject violence into a fairy
tale. In "The Willful Child," a young girl refuses to obey her
mother. God is not pleased with such blatant disobedience.
God curses the child with sickness and death. Glad to be rid
of her, the family drops her into the ground and shovels dirt
upon her. Does the child rest in peace? No. She stretches her
arm out in retaliation. More dirt on her. Her arm once again
rises in retaliation. Finally, the mother picks up a shovel and
whacks that arm so hard, it withdraws into the earth. The
entire bloodline, living and dead, can now rest in peace.

As a woman who stayed in the convent for twenty-
four years and more often than not felt the misfit, I relate
to Grimm's fable. *If I got through the novitiate, I can get through
anything.* Where had I buried the enthusiasm for the journey?
More importantly, where had I discarded the humility, gratitude, and obedience? The month before making my public
commitment was the perfect time—not to move on—but to
move out. Free to change my mind and put my arm down, I
could have tunneled a way to another life. I didn't make that
choice. I stayed.

A mentor once said, "Sister, return to an event, but
imagine a difference." The new scene still kept the music
and the candles, but added a twist: under the watchful Eye of
God, hand shaking, candle blinking dangerously, I declared
myself unfit. Thanking the sisters for their gifts of silence

and music, labor and discipline, I handed the candle to Sister John Aloysius, and walked out of chapel—shaved head
and all—ready to climb another hill. Christ's runaway bride
scurried back to the world.

I may not have the energy and enthusiasm of the past, but I
am ready to re-examine old dreams and regrets. I think back
to my adulation of Tom Dooley. Later I discovered that he,
like many workers in Laos and Vietnam, was an informant
for the CIA. In addition, reports noted that the doctor often
had his own best interests at heart. Colleagues resented his
arrogant belief that he singlehandedly thwarted the communists. Tom Dooley accomplished much good by establishing
a clinic for people desperately in need of medical assistance,
but free of self-will he was not. He was a limited human being like the rest of us.

And what about dear, dead Chauncey? Lately I've read
how best to befriend and tend canaries. Directly under photos of yellow-crowned heads lifted in song is this information: canaries need to fly. Studies of canary behavior show
that these songbirds need several hours a day out of the cage.
Free flight allows a canary to build muscles, burn energy,
and be stimulated by a world outside an enclosure. Sac mites,
cigarette smoke, or canary pox may have led to my feathered
friend's demise, but not freedom.

Releasing my beloved bird did not weaken him and did
not kill him. Chauncey needed to spread his wings. Now my
avoidance of zoos and hatred of cages makes sense. Those
who tie a bird's small claw with a cord—whether slender or

thick—strip them of the gift imprinted on their nature: free flight.

For years I avoided returning to the written words of Romano Guardini. I feared the disappointment and the inevitable scolding I would give myself. *Look at all the years you wasted thinking Dooley was a saint and Chauncey was ruined by your disobedience. What makes you think you understood Guardini?* I did not want a memory of God's will to turn trickster. I bought a copy of *The Living God*, but did not open it for months. Finally, my heart more tranquil and Angel asleep on her cushion, I sat in my bedroom chair and began to read.

The Living God resonated as truly as it did when I was twenty. God's will is not a set of orders but a path God prepares under our feet. If we digress into the underbrush, God does not frown, but adjusts, creating the path anew beneath our mud-caked boots. We are partners with the Lord of the Universe. God watches us, God walks with us. God sees us. And God's vision does not regard us with disappointment, only with love. In God's sight we become our best and truest self.

Romano Guardini's theology warms my jaded soul and transports it back to a small chapel on Palatine Hill where, through stained glass, the sun shone on innocence.

In the past I have blamed the Franciscan congregation for not recognizing I was a misfit. That is unfair. No one chained me to religious life, no barbed wire trapped me, and no bars caged me. I simply refused to explore in any depth this truth: neither the common life nor the enclosure suited me. I held tight to my independent will, lifted my wings, and took flight. Sure that I had embarked on the truer odyssey, I expected the sisters in my order to follow my lead. Each time I looked over my shoulder, the community seemed farther away. I thought, *Don't they realize that I know best? That I have the most accurate compass? They'd need to hurry if they want to catch up.* Not until too late did I notice that the community had taken a different road, traveling just fine without me.

Once a canary flies too far from home, the experts tell us, it's difficult if not impossible to ever lure the songbird back into a cage.

Begin Again

That they give an account of what they have done,
candidly mentioning the places in which they have
been, and the persons with whom they have con-
versed.

Evening: moments to reflect upon the day as well as the journey that took me far from home, into a life inspiring and disillusioning, expansive and confining. Each year of my novitiate reinforced my position within the Catholic Church and its centuries-old culture of religious life. If the sacrifice of my family and the vows pledged in community seemed an ill fit, I had the rituals of silence, prayer, music, study, and work that bestowed a sense of belonging and contentment. My travels, worth the cost, have brought me to places of learning and loss. Yet a gap needs still to be filled—one last stretch to find my footing.

I seek a life arc, like the golf ball rising over a Pendleton field. What remains is to gather the balls that bounced and gained yardage and then disappeared. They exist as bright

spheres—the ones my father painted red to make them easy
to find on snowy days—weighted with memories from my
1964 first vows to my exit from the Franciscans in 1985. This
evening, the scenes rest under the stars. Tomorrow, at day
break, I will collect them, let them grow warm in the palm
of my hand. On the top of memory's slope, among the weeds
and a few wildflowers, perhaps I will understand, with new
depth, how I traveled from there to here and back again.

In 1966, two years after my profession, I enjoyed freedom as
a full-fledged sister at Palatine Hill. No longer pummeled by
teaching third-graders in Southern California, I was back for
a year of study in English literature and a daily hour alone
in the gymnasium. On summer evenings, I could have been
in the community room with the rest of the sisters, enjoying
the scent of roses wafting through the open French doors
and listening to pinochle cards snap and knitting needles
click. Instead I chose the quiet, dark space of the gym.

The ritual was familiar: I removed my shoes, socks, and
celluloid collar. The floor of vinyl tiles felt firm and cool
beneath my feet, the long habit floating and loose. Behind
the stage curtain I pulled out *Andy Williams* from the stack
of LPs, turned on the record player. In the large, empty gym,
I danced.

The contract and release bent and shifted me. My neck
muscles loosened and stress flowed down my arms and out
through my fingertips. How many times had I moved with
"Moon River," wider than any mile? In a space all my own,
with music lifting and dropping me in a wave, I released

myself from ties of community obligations and family worries. Too soon, the hour would be over, and I would be Sister Miriam Michael again, the responsible student and committed nun. Those evenings in the gym, though, I was child on a raft, arms wide open, unafraid of the rapids ahead.

In 1971, on an early Saturday morning in Spokane, Washington, and alone in the school auditorium, my feet moved again, and my mind turned somersaults. Five months after final vows, I should have been settled. Instead I had the burden of a choreography for the junior high play. I had the oven to clean and lesson plans to finish. And why had I relegated my love life to the whims of thirteen-year-olds? How pathetic was that?

Focus, I told myself. Make *Oliver* a hit. Show them what you can do.

I took off my shoes, as I had done before. I felt my bare feet firm on the wood floor. The LP spun and the beat of "Consider Yourself" pulled me in. I closed my eyes, imagined the circle of dancers, the ripple effect—each picking the pocket of the one in front. Mid-twirl I made a mental note to get handkerchiefs.

Hop, step back, and step forward. The melody and words guided me into a whirl, hand clap, leap. Hands on hips, twist to the right, twist to the left, dip, turn. I leaped once more, a bit higher. Arms outstretched, I felt my body a tad off-kilter. In the air, I tried to align myself. My foot turned. The fall happened in slow-motion. Not the impact. A bone cracked in my foot. I sat on the floor, crying with pain and imagining the next eight weeks on crutches. So like me to leap into the unknown without checking my balance. Maybe the kids would write happy notes on the cast.

In 1977, two years after the death of my father, I found my-self in an Italian pensione. Tomorrow would be my last day in Assisi. The hillside home of St. Francis had been mine for one month, and how I would miss walking along the stone streets and through the gates, climbing Mt. Subasio's lush slopes and the caves far above the Spoleto Valley. I could not imagine an Oregon setting equal to midnights of moon and gelato in the piazza. Recorded opera would have to substi-tute for listening to the spill of Italian in the restaurant and shops. And were any of the nuns I knew as entertaining as the one who managed the pensione? In full habit she took her regular smoke breaks and shared hotel gossip. I would miss the Spirit of Francis who slipped into this nun's merry eyes, into geranium baskets, and into candles burning in the Portiuncula—Francis' beloved chapel that stands like a lop-sided dollhouse within the vast Santa Maria degli Angeli, the Basilica of Saint Mary of the Angels.

With my departure imminent, I felt at a loss. I would miss Francis in his Assisi as I missed my father. Charles Kennedy would have laughed at my comparing him to the Saint. One had no Italian blood and the other had no Irish. Nevertheless, they both clung to grand dreams. Disappoint-ment wounded them and illness stripped them bare.

My eyes stung at the thought of leaving. More than Damien of Molokai, even more intensely than Father Hayes,

St. Francis invited me to follow in the footsteps of Jesus. His letters and prayers, his Testament, the Admonitions and the legends—part fact, part allegory—pulsed with beauty and challenge. "Where there is Peace and Contemplation there is neither Care nor Restlessness." I memorized those words. I had been on the run for years—stationed seven different places—and often discontented. My luggage, leaning against the wall, sat ready for the trip back to the convent.

At the Jesuit retreat house in Portland, Oregon, in 1978, I sat across from my handsome, holy spiritual director. The room was small with one window. Shelves packed with books reminded retreatants to read Merton and Courtney Murray, Nouwen and Rahner. The dark, lean priest, sitting in a chair facing me, had been my guide through scripture readings and the Sufi enneagram. It should have been the perfect retreat and an affirmation of my calling. I should have given thanks for my life. The congregation had been more than generous: visits home, release from the classroom, spiritual direction, choices of postgraduate study, a thirty-day retreat, and the month in Assisi.

"If I am so fortunate," I asked the retreat priest, "why am I still restless? Why am I critical? Why am I not grateful?" I kept my voice low, my emotions under control.

He created a steeple with his hands. "Sister Antoinette, would you like to think about your vocation?" He watched my face. "Whether or not religious life is where you belong?"

On summer trips to the Oregon coast, I would dip my bare feet into the ocean. The icy water invariably shocked me—nature's slap of reality. That was my reaction to the priest's gentle question. I'd already made my final profession. I'd been a good nun. I was vocation director, for God's sake. Leave the convent? I couldn't imagine that. Where would I go?

"No, Father." I felt a tightness gather right at my breast-bone. "That is not the problem."

He nodded and suggested passages from the prophet Isaiah. I left the room, sick at heart. I possessed neither the energy nor desire to pray with Isaiah's early, passionate, "Send me!" In my room, I sat with scripture opened in my lap and let sadness—stored long inside—bleed out. I opened to Isaiah, but chose the passages where God promises not to extinguish the flickering wick or smash the fragile reed.

In spring of 1979, I was still vocation director, still recruiting, still giving retreats. Weariness from the travel sapped me, but so did disillusionment with what I perceived as the order's refusal to change. Relieved as I was to be back at Palatine Hill, I dreaded having to make conversation with the sisters. I had a couple of hours by myself plus a little reward: two Snickers bars and a bag of peanut M&Ms. When a knock sounded on the door of my room, I sighed and hid the candy under the pillow.

Sister Marjorie stood outside. Although I invited her in, the visit surprised me. We had both graduated from St. Jo-seph's Academy, but she was four years older, and our paths rarely had crossed. In addition, she held a position of pres-tige that placed her out of my small circle of friends: she was intelligent and objective, a provincial and general council member, had a PhD in urban studies, and she had lived a year at the Catholic Worker House in New York City. What in the world did she want?

"I've been talking to the provincial about an experimental community. We'd live among the poor." She hesitated. "Would you be interested?"

I said yes, delighted by some place new, complimented by the invitation.

Describing "a group of no more than four," Sister Marjorie wanted to live like Francis of Assisi, in a community of equals with no local superior and as sisters to our neighbors. Together we would decide our common goals.

When she left, my imagination flapped wings and away I flew: of course, I would be an asset. No one knew St. Francis as well as I did. And freedom to make our own way! We would be a modern-day Assisi, and the four of us would be a model for religious communities. A mountaintop city, Jesus said. I did a quick little jive, singing that line from *Godspell* about being the light that stays pretty in the city of God.

I pulled the candy from under my pillow, ate it all, and curled up for a nap.

In 1982, after one year in a low-income neighborhood and two years at the Rich Hotel in downtown Portland, I was spent. The city noise and the vitriol of the marginal had wound within me, tight as a mummy, a similar fury. When the position of director of religious education opened at St.

Stephens Indian Mission in Wyoming, I grabbed the opportunity. Far away and different.

Along with the unblinking land and people, came the invitation to the four nuns at the mission to share a "sweat" to
celebrate a young woman's sixteenth birthday. The ceremony, I learned, was a rite of reconciliation—a hot one. Advice?
Wear scant, loose clothing and no metal. An Arapaho elder,
his eyes wise and amused, said, "Breathe into the heat."

On a February afternoon, clad in a tank top and shorts, I
shivered in the winter snow, waiting to enter the sweat lodge,
a low-slung igloo set behind a private home. We slipped out
of our shoes and filed into the small lodge, first the men
and then the women—seventeen of us crammed into a space
meant to hold no more than six. Body to body we sat in a
circle, cross-legged, inches away from a pile of heated stones
while the Indian men joked in Arapaho with the two Jesuit priests. Outside the opened flap, snow-covered ground
stretched to the base of the mountains. The sky was as blue
as a winter Wyoming day could be.

Then one of the men dropped the flap and daylight ended.

At that moment, I could have channeled the courage of
Powder Face or Little Raven, Arapaho chiefs who refused to
retreat. Instead I morphed into Edgar Allen Poe's Fortunato
sealed in a tomb. I dropped headlong into dread. I wanted to
escape, but could not shame myself by crawling over bodies.
Encased in fear and so close to heat that I smelled its texture,
I chose to burn rather than quit. As the ceremony progressed,
I gasped for air. The woman next to me thrust a clump of
sage into my hand. "Breathe, it will help." I brought the stiff

plant close to my nose, and the pungent odor startled and revived me. But not for long.

When the water dipper made its rounds and I had to pour some on the ground for Mother Earth, I fumed, trapped where I did not want to be. The leader poured water over the rocks once, twice, three times. I felt his eyes on me, his mockery. I would not quit. I would stick it out, even if I fainted. The flap opened and the winter air cooled me and I rested for one minute, then two.

The flap closed again.

Steam and heat spat and hissed. I bent my head and pulled at my hair, dry and brittle strands that would snap like wheat. I wrung the bottom of my tank top. I squeezed out one measly drop. Muscles screamed for relief, for one gust of cool air. Open the flap, I wanted to cry. For God's sake, open the flap.

Ernest's words returned: "Breathe into the heat." With no other option, I did as I was told.

Heat scalded my throat and seared my lungs. "Let go," I whispered to myself. Moisture licked my scalp. Water escaped, a trickle, but I felt it roll through my hair and slide down my face. Miracle of miracles, from every pore flowed sweat, salty and delicious.

The flap opened. I had endured. As I lay on my back in the igloo, breathing in the winter air, Wyoming's blue sky and mountains turned upside down.

By 1984, two years later, I felt trapped once more. I felt less and less connected with my religious community, Church hierarchy, and tribal leaders. Once again, I sought a way out. Maybe that's why I agreed to Sister Mary's birthday trip up the Sinks Canyon. The weekend trek would wind around limestone and foothills, all the way into an alpine forest. The problem? We would travel by horseback. Blotting out any vision of S'mores under starlight was an inner scream: *Are you kidding? The last horse you rode was a carousel pinto.*

We arrived at the canyon, but drove higher until we arrived at the parking lot. The men opened the trailer, and my mount shuffled out: Sheila, seventeen hands high and pregnant.

After a fuss with a saddle and a hoist up onto her back, I was on my way—sort of. No matter how I urged her, Sheila poked along. Six members of the group moved up the canyon at a fast trot, but Mary, whose horse proved equally recalcitrant, lagged behind with me. We did get the horses into the open, and up one slope and then another, but we were still far behind. "Maybe we should turn back," I said.

As if to answer, Mary pointed to a spot high up the canyon. I followed her finger to see a horse kick, buck, and fling its rider like a cloth toy. Instantly, the overloaded pack horses spun and galloped downhill straight toward us. Mary's horse reared. Phlegmatic Sheila burst into life. She did not head back toward the parking lot, but after the other horses, down, down into the heart of the canyon. She strained at the reins and hurtled, out of control, after the runaway horses. I clung to one certainty: If I hang on, I'll die. I released the reins, took a deep breath, whispered, "Geronimo," and rolled off the galloping horse. The unkind ground whammed me—

hard. The riders galloped toward us and a woman cried out, "Oh, my God! Oh my God!"

I moved my arms and legs. "I'm fine," I yelled.

"Not you," she cried. "Mary!"

I turned to see my friend, lying on the ground, her head split open.

Gutsy lady that she was, Mary refused to lose consciousness. She asked about the horses and smiled when she learned they were safe. She endured forty stitches and later joked about a birthday like no other.

Not me. I cursed myself for agreeing to a venture alien to my skill set. I blamed the leader for burdening the pack horses and seethed at his public reprimand. "Never let go of a runaway horse. You should have ridden her down the canyon." *Should have? Should have?* "You quit," he said.

He was right about that. I refused to hang on until death parted us. Instead, I figured that since I wasn't going up, I wasn't going down either. And know what? Even though I never made it up to the top of the canyon, I had accomplished the unexpected. Quitting turned into a gold coin tucked in a pocket for safekeeping—just in case.

In autumn of 1984, in an office in Casper, Wyoming, I sat with my journal open. Across from me was a Jungian therapist who was helping me deal with estrangement from my sisters and colleagues. We explored my childhood and likeness to my father. This day, though, she wanted me to examine something else.

"Tell me again about your recurring dream," she said.

"I'm watching a young Indian trapped under an overpass. He wears a headband and no shirt over his slim, muscular body. His buckskin leggings have tassels that move, and his feet are bare. I see him caught in mid-motion. He's frightened by the trucks rumbling above him and the traffic around him. His face is strained. He is lost. I watch him and want to help him get home. I try to call to him, but no words come. I am heartbroken that he can't hear me. Then I wake up."

The therapist nodded and said, "Antoinette, let's explore your call to religious life."

A retreat director, seven years ago, had opened up the same possibility. Defensive and fearful, I had not listened. That day in a Wyoming office, I did not restate my fine qualities or noble motives, nor did I argue with her. It was time.

In 1985, on an early summer day in Portland, Oregon, I climbed the stairs to the Archdiocesan Chancery Office on East Burnside Street. In a large, airy conference room two priests, black suits pressed, shoes shined, stood, deep in conversation. Father Greg turned, and his boyish face broke into a smile. "Good to see you, Sister." He asked how I'd been and when I had last visited Father Alan. Without even an eyebrow raised in judgment, he asked, "Are you here for your dispensation papers?" I nodded.

Father Greg picked up a folder on his desk. I sat at a conference table and with a black ball point pen, signed my way out of religious life, and returned the papers. Father Greg smiled, shook my hand, and wished me well.

How simple the process—nothing like the movie, *The Nun's Story*, the gloomy scene when Sister Luke leaves her community. No silent stone corridors, no disappointed superior refusing eye-contact, no exchange of the flowing habit for a dress two sizes too large, and no oak doors shutting tight behind me. Instead, a welcome and a farewell from a great-hearted priest who wouldn't know how to hold a grudge. No drama, simply a document, a signature, a date, a descent down concrete steps into sunlight, and a stop at a coffee shop for a cup of hot chocolate with whipped cream.

As a now outdated theology would have termed it, I left the world years ago and now I was returning to it.

I watch the maple that grows outside my bedroom window. What a miracle that the tree flushes green in summer, blazes orange and red in autumn, stretches fingers toward the sky in winter, and leafs again in spring. Like the tree we transform. We leave and return. Place us like the maple in any season. It doesn't matter. We will come full circle and begin again.

Starting from anywhere is where I am, still walking barefoot across a rickety bridge. I've had my share of travel under stern skies and soaring evergreens. I've looked down on raging waters and dipped tired feet in streams, climbed switchbacks in the dark and stumbled over rocks. If today the path is more level and my pace not so urgent, I am, nevertheless, part of the story told in Lindberg's painting *Heilige Schutzengel*—the child on an adventure. One guardian angel walks behind, and another—Angel, my Shih Tzu—struts ahead.

Songbirds twitter in flight, maybe a thrush or two heading thousands of miles to the south. I'm free to take any path, but for now I find my way along a well-trod, shadow-dappled road: one of God's restless, romantic creations, forever yearning to be somewhere else.

More from Fuze Publishing

Entering the Blue Stone by Molly Best Tinsley
The General battles Parkinson's; his wife manifests a bizarre dementia. Their grown children embrace what seems a solution—an upscale retirement community. Between laughter and dismay, discover what shines beneath catastrophe: family bonds, the dignity of even an unsound mind, and the endurance of the heart. *Memoir*

How the Winds Laughed by Addie Greene
When Addie Greene and her young husband take on the "great adventure" of circumnavigation in a 28-foot boat, a succession of catastrophes demands that she become the driving force in carrying them forward and safely home. *Memoir*

The Gift of El Tio by Larry Buchanan and Karen Gans
When a world-renowned geologist discovers an enormous deposit of silver beneath a remote Quechua village in Bolivia, he unknowingly fulfills a 450-year-old prophecy that promised a life of wealth for the villagers. *Memoir*

Nobody Knows the Spanish I Speak by Mark Saunders

High-tech couple from Portland, Oregon, emigrates with large dog and ornery cat to San Miguel de Allende, in the middle of Mexico. Their well-intentioned cluelessness makes for mayhem and nonstop laughs. *Memoir*

Black Wings by Kathleen Jabs

Lieutenant Bridget Donovan battles Navy hierarchy to find the truth behind the tragic plane crash of one of the Navy's first female combat pilots, Audrey Richards, Bridget's Academy roommate. Bridget's life is at stake when she uncovers the warped code of honor behind a secret Academy group. *Fiction*

Cologne by Sarah Pleydell

London, 1960. Renate von Hasselmann, an au pair escaping postwar Germany, takes charge of precocious Caroline and Maggie Whitaker. The girls' debonair father disarms the young woman with his quicksilver charm, childhood collides with history, and the traumas of war are visited upon the children of the peace. *Fiction*

Leaving Tuscaloosa by Walter Bennett

1962. Racial turmoil in the deep South engulfs two estranged boyhood friends, one black and one white. Veering from the heat of erotic passion to the spreading fires of racial violence, their paths converge in a moving, shocking climax. *Fiction*

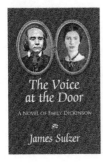

The Voice at the Door by James Sulzer

A fictional account of the iconic American poet that explores the secret behind Emily Dickinson's agonized love poetry of the early 1860s—her fateful meeting with the famous Philadelphia pastor, Charles Wadsworth. *The Voice at the Door* brings to new life Dickinson's intelligence, naïveté, eccentricity, passion, and sly humor. *Fiction*